The
Betrayal of Intellect
in Higher Education

The
Betrayal of Intellect in Higher Education

Mohammed Mujeeb Rahman

OMNIVIEW PUBLISHING
TORONTO

Canadian Cataloguing in Publication Data
Rahman, Mohammed Mujeeb 1937 -
    The betrayal of intellect in higher education

Includes bibliographical references and index.

ISBN 0-9682479-0-3

1. Education, Higher - Canada. 2. Education, Higher - United States. I. Title.

LB2322.R3 1997   378.71   C97-931495-X

Printed and bound in Canada

Dedicated to

All Academics – Professors & Students
Who
Endorse the idea of Liberal Education
and
Espouse the ideals of intellectual freedom and integrity

Man is only born ignorant. It takes four years of college to make him stupid.
- Mark Twain
Wit and Wisdom

We are faced with the paradoxical fact that education has become one of the chief obstacles to intelligence and freedom of thought.
- Bertrand Russell
Sceptical Essays

We live in a world that is not merely unintellectual but anti-intellectual as well. Even the universities are anti-intellectual.
- Robert Maynard Hutchins
The Higher Learning in America

In theory and practice alike, then, and from top to bottom, American education serves other ends than Intellect.
- Jacques Barzun
The House of Intellect

Contents

· ·

Preface

This book was conceived ten years ago soon after publication of my previous book *The Psychological Quest: From Socrates to Freud* in 1987, which focused on the historical amnesia that modern academic psychology has displayed towards the great philosophical and literary works that embody many deep insights into human nature. As was also noted at the time, such historical amnesia was simply a reflection of the wider academic ethos. That same year was marked by a momentous event that literally shook the academic world to its core – the publication of Allan Bloom's book *The Closing of the Academic Mind*. This proved to be the catalyst that opened my already prepared mind to the possibility of further examination of the many fads and foibles of modern university education, beyond the brief and scattered comments in my earlier book – only a handful of which also seemed quite appropriate for inclusion here and there in this book.

Although a major portion of the first draft of this book was completed during my sabbatical in 1990, it has still taken ten years from conception to publication – with much of the work of revision spread out over the yearly summer breaks, as I periodically tried to tie up as many loose ends as possible in order to assure both the reasonableness and consistency of the whole argument. Those ideas and conceptual distinctions that were vital to the present discussion also underwent a process of continual critical evaluation during this rather extended passage of time – until I was satisfied that they were viable enough to progress from manuscript to publication. While the seven years from first to final draft may seem unusually long for this book, the unavoidable delays in the final stages of publishing have taken more than a fair share of that time.

Yet, short as the book has finally turned out to be for something in this genre, it is nevertheless based on several years of reading and reflection, coupled with patient observations of programs, policies and people in various universities over the years. Thus even those generalizations that may appear somewhat categorical due to their brevity are a result of considerable deliberation. Controversial as they may seem, I do believe that the generalizations, conceptual distinctions and arguments presented here will shed some light on the current crisis in higher education. That some heat may also be generated in the process is almost inevitable. Unfortunately, sweetness and light cannot always be united – *pace* Matthew Arnold.

I know that I cannot expect to be easily forgiven for my depiction of the dismal state of affairs in academia, but I can only remind the reader that it would be very difficult for anyone to undertake a book-length critique of the university system without caring for it deeply. That this book is seeing the light of print on the eve of my retirement* is entirely coincidental, and not due to any intention on my part to go into hiding – much as that too may have been the better part of academic wisdom!

Stratford
Prince Edward Island
March 1997

---

* The eve of retirement may well have become the morning after by the time the book is released from the press.

Controversia in Academia

If liberty means anything at all, it means the right to tell people what they do not want to hear.

- George Orwell
Introduction,* Animal Farm

There have been many occasions during my three and a half decades of university teaching when I felt compelled to exercise the liberty to tell university colleagues and administrators what they would rather not have wanted to hear. The many candidly critical articles and epistles I have written over the years have piled up into what some academics would undoubtedly brand as 'satanic prose.' While putting a price on my head would have been pushing it a bit, it would not have surprised me to know if that, too, was considered in some scholarly circles!

That I am alive and well, and happily retired in fairly good health, testifies to the high value placed on the principle of academic freedom. In practice, however, speaking the truth about academic pretensions is fraught with high risk and is incompatible with smooth career advancement. Yet, for those who still continue to believe that truth can neither be economized nor compromised, there is really no other choice – except to abandon all hope for peace and prosperity as they enter the polemical life in the hallowed halls of academe. Personally speaking, I have found solace in the sentiment expressed by an eminent president of Harvard University: "I was never lonely; I always had a fight on my hands."

While this book may seem to have been written in a combative spirit, it merely reflects a profound sense of concern with what seems to pass for higher education today in a majority of universities across North America. Since education is as subject to globalization as the economy, there is no doubt that at least some of the concerns raised here may well be applicable in varying degrees to university education elsewhere in the world.

What my book adds to the ongoing debate on the fate of higher education is but a small voice – a kind of afterword to the works of all those distinguished critics whose views I have shared over the years, and whose thoughts and words I also share herein with the readers. Briefly re-visiting the evaluations and exhortations of some of the earlier critics in the course of our examination clearly shows that we have really not come a long way at all, either in our diagnosis or our prescriptions. It will be obvious to the reader that old wine in the original bottles still has enough spiritual food for thought and action. However, despite my perception of affinity, as well as several points of similarity, it is possible that even some of these earlier critics may not necessarily share all my observations and conclusions. Yet, I do believe that most of them would endorse the general thrust of my critique, which focuses mainly on the plight of the intellect in the academic world. The pressing importance of this problem makes it imperative for us to continue to raise disturbing questions, even if we are unable to offer all the right answers.

That all the diagnostic and prescriptive acumen already available has not been heeded to the extent that it deserves may mean that the fast pace of change and information turnover is leaving both thought and talk so far behind that most of the critical commentaries appear to have become more like obituaries. Given such a record, there is no reason to believe that a better fate awaits the present critique. Realistically, therefore, it is almost impossible to avoid some skeptical intimations in the course of our musings on the future of higher education. Idealistically, of course, hope seems to spring eternal – at least in some academic breasts. Critical books on the subject continue to be written under the philosophy of "as if" – as if they make a difference. Authors of such books may therefore be forgiven for periodically allowing their hope to triumph over all the experience that indicates otherwise.

Although it is said that the sting of criticism is often a measure of its truth, a cautionary note may still be in order for those who wish to exercise their liberty not to hear what may be academically unpalatable. It would therefore be prudent to include a forewarning to the effect that various politically incorrect portions of this book may cause varying levels of academic uneasiness. Thus some degree of reader-discretion may well be advised.

Prologue

The university is too important to be taken for granted. It needs constant critical analysis.

- Claude Bissell
The University Game

With few exceptions, academics seem to take the university for granted. However, universities are not sacred cows exempt from being subjected to critical examination. Critical inquiry is, of course, the very life-blood of a university; where there is too much complacency, a university degenerates into a bureaucracy. Prolonged disuse of academic freedom devalues it, dulls its critical edge, and leaves it without any critical substance. What remains then is simply an illusion of academic freedom.

It is incumbent upon us, therefore, to honor the Socratic legacy, and to follow the example of the gadfly in never passing up an opportunity to exercise our critical faculties. An uncritical academic life, like an unexamined one, is not worth living – since the promotion of critical thought and the pursuit of truth are the very reasons for the existence of our venerable institutions of higher education.

What follows is simply an attempt to examine the academic life in the critical spirit of that ancient legacy – however painful it may be to face the truth. For, like Aristotle, we too can say that piety requires us to honor truth above our friends; and if we are to resolutely seek truth in the groves of academe as Horace enjoined us to do, then we must be prepared, with Augustine, to love truth whether it reveals itself or ourselves; all that it takes is what Nietzsche called the courage for an attack on our convictions.

A Note on "Liberal Arts" & "Liberal Education"

The *liberal arts* were first outlined in Plato's *Republic* as skills proper to free persons. Liberal arts were also part of the educational curriculum of medieval universities. In this original form they comprised the verbal arts of the trivium (grammar, logic and rhetoric), and the mathematical arts of the quadrivium (arithmetic, geometry, astronomy and music). These seven arts were considered to provide the basic skills for the study of the humanities, the sciences and mathematics.

While "liberal arts" are sometimes used narrowly to refer only to the humanities (which accounts for the expression "liberal arts and sciences"), most universities today use that phrase broadly with reference to academic programs that are not specifically vocational, but provide different levels of specialized knowledge and research experience in a variety of academic subjects: philosophy, history, classics, literature, languages, fine arts, mathematics, and the natural and social sciences. In practice, the majority of post-secondary multiversities offer a broad spectrum of diverse programs that include not only an assortment of academic specialties, but also varying combinations of professional, technical, vocational and practical service programs, which may differ from one university to another.

As used in this book, *liberal education* is differentiated not only from such utilitarian programs, but also from any kind of education based on a research-specialist orientation to the various academic disciplines. What characterizes true liberal education is its generalist-humanist approach to knowledge, which is based on a historically grounded study of the great works and ideas in the humanities and sciences for the sole purpose of cultivating general intellectual ability. This 'liberal' aspect is viewed here as the key feature of higher education, in contrast to the 'specialist' and 'utilitarian' aspects of the many prevalent forms of post-secondary education.

Chapter 1

• •

The Decline and Fall
of Higher Education

By and large the present universities do not and cannot educate.
- Paul Goodman
The Community of Scholars[1]

Academic life can often seem like a comedy to those who care to think about it honestly. The very solemnity with which some of the sacred cows of academia are paraded before the public invites laughter. However, this irreverent examination of such academic pomposities is only meant to provoke thought, not to promote laughter – much as that too may be needed to prod the bovine elements out of the groves of academe.

Ideally speaking, the purpose of higher education is to cultivate the mind by a course of study which promotes sound habits of learning, inquiry, independent judgment, critical thought and creative imagination. The ideal outcome of higher education is the development of competence in the pursuit and integration of knowledge, an understanding of the significant ideas that have shaped modern knowledge and human history, an appreciation of the great works of human intellect and imagination, and an abiding interest in enhancing one's knowledge, understanding, and wisdom. The chief value of higher education lies in our being able to find pleasure in exercising our minds on the goods of the mind, for the good of the mind.

Many critical observers of the academic scene recognize that such ideals of higher education are not being well-served by the majority of our colleges and universities, while knowledge, understanding and wisdom have all been lost in a mass of uncoordinated facts and specialized forms of information which permeate and subvert most academic programs today.

The pervasive emphasis on over-specialized knowledge and on research techniques, especially in the early years of higher education, has created generalized ignorance and the learned ignoramus. The enormous capital of intelligence and talent in the halls of academe continues to be wastefully invested in diversified specialisms, resulting in a fragmented curriculum which imposes a premature specialization that has as little edifying value as the occupationally relevant and politically correct courses. Knowledge, understanding and wisdom can hardly be expected to prevail in such an academic context.

Uncensored reflection on the present state of academic affairs leads to at least four plausible observations:

1. Most universities have become unfit places for higher education.
2. Most academic programs do more harm than good to the intellect.
3. Most universities care more for academic productivity and for the enhancement of bureaucracy than for the real educational needs of students.
4. Most academic degrees are little more than certificates of university attendance and course credits.

To also suggest at this stage that most of these problems may have inadvertently resulted from increased funding in the past would be to provoke among the inhabitants of an already beleaguered academy a round of both tears and laughter – such as would result from a combination of sodium and nitrous oxide, suddenly and simultaneously injected into the orifices and gashes of an already wounded being. Nevertheless, such a paradoxical possibility must be examined at some point, even at the risk of further drying up the udders of one of the sacred cows of academia. Excess funding in the past may have actually been hazardous to higher education.

Shocking as such irreverent observations may seem, it is necessary to reflect on them in any critical examination of academic institutions. Meanwhile, it may be prudent to prevent our academic illusions from getting in the way of a candid diagnosis of university education.

꙾— II —꙾

Critical thought, the pursuit of truth, and excellence in scholarship constitute the trinity of academic objectives advertised by most universities in their mission statements. Of course, those who combine honesty with the courage to see through the academic accouterments realize that such publicized objectives represent rhetoric more than the reality of modern academic institutions.

In our age of commercialism, colleges and universities have quickly learned that, like other business enterprises, they too are in the business of selling images to the consumers of the knowledge industry – even when such images are not consistent with the actual products offered. Dangling unrealistic promises before an unsuspecting public, purely for purposes of enticement, would constitute false advertising – if universities and colleges were classified as businesses, rather than as public service institutions. Like politicians, therefore, universities also seem to get away by covering up a modest performance with a glorified image. Such commercialized double talk remains inconsistent with the pursuit of truth advertised by most academic institutions as their raison d'être. As one perceptive student put it in a recent national survey: "Universities talk about giving students critical thinking skills, mental flexibility, value-added this and that. Then they want to set them loose on the Internet, give them an e-mail address, and call it higher education."[2]

It is tricky business indeed for modern universities to maintain the appearance of pursuing the traditional objectives of education, even as they continue to dismantle the remnants of liberal education programs – long considered to be the hallmark of excellence in higher education. Perhaps the pomp and ceremony of the annual graduation exercises create the illusion that universities are indeed the repositories of knowledge and the founts of wisdom, where critical and creative thought flows freely in the fearless and objective pursuit of truth and excellence.

Much of the confusion of tongues in academia in this regard seems to reflect the ambiguity with which excellence is bandied about. "Excellence does not come cheaply" one learned academic said in a convocation address, apparently referring to the high cost of high-tech equipment. Then, in almost the next academically amnesic breath, added that the best things in life like "honor, love and the soul of man, cannot be bought at any price." Nor can excellence in education be bought, since its spiritual goods like truth, beauty and goodness, are also priceless – and accessible only to passion and commitment, not to affluence. Likewise, another academic sophisticate noted that "universities do indeed train for jobs, and do perform research beneficial to industry" but that "somewhere in itself, [they] must be concerned with learning."[3] As oratory, this may pass as a solemn comment at a ceremonial event. Upon sober reflection, however, one can see not only confusion, but comical implications. At least one is left wondering whether this means that training for jobs and research for industry do not involve learning, or that some learning must also be squeezed in somehow during the time remaining after job-training and research. Even simple reflection seems to suggest that terms like excellence and learning signify levels of achievement in all sorts of areas and activities from plumbing to professional bartending – not all of which are appropriate in an academic curriculum. It is, therefore, not very edifying to use these terms so carelessly even for purposes of inspirational oratory, without first identifying the object of excellence or the subject of learning.

There are other examples of trendy academic slogans which have no more than a pleasant ring to them. For instance, the solemn declarations that universities be 'student-centered,' which, in a sense, they already are by definition – in the same way that, by definition, hospitals are patient-centered. However, such pious proclamations, despite their emptiness, do seem to betray a collective academic guilt about the inordinate amount of time many faculty spend on specialized research, wasteful committee work, and campus politics – at the expense of teaching. It would seem far more appropriate, therefore, to express the underlying concern by affirming that universities need to be teaching-cum-scholarship centered, first and foremost – although even this should be true by definition, were it not for the other non-teaching obligations which are pursued with more gusto than guilt for their career advancement value.

What all this makes obvious is the fact that we are either confused about what our words have come to mean, or we are confused about the basic ends of education – which, in turn, leads to confused policies resulting in an incoherent curriculum. In any case, in the interest of right thought, right speech, and right action, it may be best to stop misguiding the students and the public, and start recognizing that universities today are not providing higher education in any meaningful sense of the term. In fact, university education has become a meaningless experience for many of those who aspire to become well-educated. No longer can we say today that it is enough to have graduated in order to be educated.

As truth is the first casualty during a war and in the course of double-talk, critical thought is the first casualty in a bureaucracy. The increase in the bureaucratization of education and scholarship is largely the result of government demands for manpower planning and accountability, and market demands for the expansion of academic goods and services. The resulting complexity of restructuring has inevitably caused a proliferation of rules and roles – including more bureaucratic roles for administrators.

Academic leadership has always required managerial skills such as business management, information management, conflict management, and impression management. However, with greater refinement and widespread application of such skills over the years, many academic managers have turned into bureaucratic functionaries with a high degree of efficiency in the fine arts of newspeak, lip-service, and paper-pushing. Such a shift in roles has completely displaced the centrality of the traditional academic vision of higher education – which remains confined to paper, and is reserved only for ceremonial occasions and public consumption. Of course, such paper vision also remains safe from being exposed as being out of touch with the institutional realities of the day.

Under the circumstances, professional appeasers with sufficient ambition, political savvy and public-relation skills have been able to rise to their level of incompetence in various leadership positions in an educational system already beset with confusion both about means and ends. Without a well-defined system to serve, talented bureaucrats have no choice but to become self-serving – thereby draining much scholarly energy into political diversions, and inevitably creating a widespread bureaucratic mind-set that is extremely hostile to intellectual life in academia. Critical thought thus gets preempted by pseudo-civility and collegiality of various decision-making bodies, whose democratic decorum approves conformist input at the expense of rational dialogue and debate. Understandably then, most academic decisions often end up being based on blatantly political considerations, rather than on the basis of a sound philosophical or educational rationale. Universities continue to be thus undermined from within by such anti-intellectual measures and bureaucratic managers. Undoubtedly, the standardization of such power-politics and practices has played a major role in destroying the unity and intellectual purpose of higher education.

Imposition of bureaucratic policies which have the merit of combining optimum efficiency with near maximum irrationality could only lead to a proliferation of specialties and a fragmented curriculum – ironically, in the name of program enrichment. The gradual elimination of liberal education programs, which provide the unifying and edifying basis of all higher education, has thus caused a serious erosion of intellectual life in academia. With a minimum of shared intellectual ideas or interests, and a virtual absence of any meaningful meeting of minds between different specialists, even within the same discipline, the very foundation for a community of scholars has disappeared – only to be replaced locally by the collegiality of committees, and globally by conferencing colleagues loyal only to their disciplines. Meanwhile, research, pedantry and gimmickry have served to enhance productivity, triviality and mediocrity at the expense of genuine creativity, knowledge and scholarship.

Bureaucratic policies and pressures thus erode scholarly communities with a shared tradition, and promote specialized collectives with myopic aims. Institutional accountability to government inevitably adulterates intrinsic intellectual values of higher education with extrinsic vocational standards suited to post-secondary training. This betrayal of intellect in higher education is further reinforced when pedagogical responsibility for the edification of future citizens also becomes a matter of accountability to institutional bureaucracy. Responsibility to the intellectual aims of higher education is thus subverted for reasons of expediency by using market values to validate the ideals of educational commitment.

Such a state of affairs could not have led to anything other than the present crisis in the halls of Academe – placing higher education itself on trial. Contrary to popular wisdom, however, such a crisis has resulted not so much from a lack of funds as from a lack of ideas, not so much from a loss of nerve as from a loss of vision. For where there is no clear vision of an authentic identity, the university must inevitably face a crisis.

The crisis of universities is thus an identity crisis which needs to be resolved if higher education is to be reinstated in our universities. Philip Rieff defines the vision of a university with his characteristic candor:

> If the university is still to be the temple of the intellect, mind entire, then its high priests can only worship the intellect, which does not worship itself. The enforcement of intellect, upon ourselves and reluctant students – that is our one force; it is to that force that we

have a duty, uniquely unchangeable. Because the university must be the temple of the intellect, uniquely unchangeable in that respect, it is a sacred institution, the last in our culture. If the university is not the temple of the intellect, then it is not a university.[4]

The traditional identity of an academy as a temple of intellect has been fragmented and parcelled out to the multiple interests that constitute the pulls and pressures of a commercially conformist society based on the laws of supply and demand. Consequently, it has become increasingly difficult to see how and why the operating principles and privileges of academia are different from those of other social institutions, businesses and government. It also becomes somewhat puzzling to find that, instead of healing with time, the crisis has only kept worsening, almost as if in utter disregard for any kind of fiscal or bureaucratic solutions. In fact, in accordance with Parkinson's law, academic needs, too, have kept expanding to use up all the funds available – even as universities continue to "impoverish the souls of today's students" as Allan Bloom argued. No redemption seems possible unless we resolve the academic identity crisis by way of identifying the quintessential aim of higher education in terms of its potential for the nurturing of intellect.

◌— III —◌

Over the years, then, both the identity of a University and the aims of education have undergone many transformations under the continuing pressures of the multiplicity of social demands, market interests, technological needs and political agendas – all of which have vied for the control of the educational curriculum. The rampant proliferation of the curriculum that came with increases in funding has inevitably led to a rapid fragmentation in the world of higher education. Where once only the humanities were at odds with the sciences, now one specialism is at odds with another – creating towers of babel, with different methodologies and disciplinary perspectives which debase thought and language into data bases and information systems of their own making. Thus it would not be too unfair to say that the university was transformed into an institutional form of a multiple personality when it became an affluent multiversity.

The ivory tower has long been a relic of the past. Even the "two cultures" constituting the university have fragmented into the "multicultural" educational mosaic of the modern multiversity with its prime emphasis on professional and specialized training and research, at the expense of liberal education. In the process, the community of scholars has finally evolved into a corporation of itinerant researchers and pedants, specialized in pursuing private interests at public expense. The esoteric publications – that are the goods and services of academic productivity – have contributed more to promoting personal careers than to advancing public knowledge. As a result, education has become overloaded with much trivial information, which is sufficiently jargonized to justify further grant appropriations by the academically incorporated hordes of researchers. As perfection of technical means became confused over time with the pursuit of educational ends, the art of teaching got degraded to scientifically measured instruction by pseudo-quantification of quality. As undergraduate education aped graduate training, liberal education became peripheral to professional, technical and vocational training – until "know-how" (technique) eventually got the better of "know-what" (content) as the ultimate value. A commercial point of view has thus become endemic in academia, as historian Erich Kahler observed:

> Education follows the current trend toward "vocational training," that is, making young people fit for advantageous careers; entertainment, the means of communication, appeal to the lowest standard of demand. How could it be otherwise in a social system that in all its parts is guided by the commercial point of view? Nothing less will do than a radical change in our whole outlook and social attitude.[5]

The gradual erosion of liberal education during the post World War II years, was a consequence of such pressured proliferation of the curriculum to accommodate the varied and competing interests residing in the social, political, business, industrial and military establishments. Scientific specialisms skyrocketed even more after the Russian Sputnik raised the American political and academic consciousness to a new level in more than a century of gradual accommodation to the needs of the industrial age. The traditional ideal of education and the idea of a university as a community of scholars, dedicated to the pursuit of knowledge, understanding and wisdom, were irrevocably transformed into the new reality of a nationalized knowledge industry, dedicated to the pursuit of industrial power, economic prosperity and political prestige.

Liberal education quickly became a lost cause in the vast expanses of the space age and the ever increasing noise of the overwhelming information age, as even the few so-called institutions of liberal education were infiltrated in varying degrees by the specialisms of the market and the industry. Under such circumstances, it would have been miraculous if short term objectives had not gained priority over long acclaimed educational ends. When ideals and dollars are in competition, lip service and bureaucratic prevarication are always on the scene to cover the gap between promise and practice. A hodgepodge of specialized training programs were thus allowed to fragment the unity of liberal education, without even the blinking of an academic eye – ironically, for the cause of promoting higher education!

The assaults from within contributed their fair share to leveling the walls of the ivory tower already besieged by the forces of the market and the industry. The politicization of the university in the sixties and the consequent flowering of the ideologies of commitment and relevance, led to the disenfranchisement of educational elitism. It seemed as if the best lacked all conviction to lead, while the most vocal of the rest were full of passionate intensity for power. More anarchy was loosed upon the academic world by the new relativism of the social sciences which, with their manipulative ideology and value equalization, provided the rhetoric and rationale for academic and intellectual egalitarianism.

Thus the university acquired its present status as an odd mixture of a research-development industry and a medley of political-ideological camps. Is it surprising then that the platitudinous mission statements of many of today's self-proclaimed liberal education institutions have no more than a hollow ring to them? Of course, everyone from the Governing Board to the bored students are supposed to play along – knowing that such lofty protestations are no more than sterile substitutes for action, meant more for public consumption than for academic inspiration.

Any attempt at healing the many problems afflicting the academic world needs to be preceded both by some conceptual clarification and by historical examination of the premises and purposes of university education. In an exploration of the meaning of 'mind' in the modern world, and the reasons for its eclipse, Lionel Trilling provides a general diagnosis which captures the essential nature of our academic malady. His penetratingly simple words also carry an implicit prescription:

> The diminished morale which marks the academic profession in its official existence is, we may suppose, of a piece with the growing intellectual recessiveness of college and university faculties, their reluctance to formulate any coherent theory of education, to discover what its best purposes are, and try to realize them through the requirements of the curriculum.[6]

The prevailing disorder in higher learning may thus be traced to a serious confusion about the purposes of education. Only the identification of such purposes can bring about some order out of the chaos which is eroding the very basis of intellectual life in academia. A critical step in this direction may lie in making a strategic conceptual distinction between higher education and post-secondary education. These terms can be used synonymously only if we choose to ignore the vital difference between what comes after secondary school education and moves us onwards, and what is higher and moves us upwards. The post-secondary education, so widely prevalent in modern universities, is all that makes for professional and specialized training designed to serve the diverse needs and demands of the various sectors of society. On the other hand, higher education is what makes for an intellectual culture of humanity – which is made possible by exposure to the knowledge of "the best that has been known and said in the world" – to use the classic expression of Matthew Arnold.

Consequently, post-secondary education, with its emphasis on current research and issues, becomes a hindrance to fostering intellectual life and to promoting the growth of culture in this received sense. Bertrand Russell's observation was to the point: "The current trend towards more and fiercer specialisms is making men forget their intellectual debts to their forbears." Ideally, higher education must aim at countering such forgetfulness. In this sense, it is not higher education which has "failed democracy" or "impoverished the souls of today's students" as Allan Bloom had put it, but our universities which have failed higher education by not countering the historical amnesia that has become so pervasive in our academic programs.[7]

The prime requirement for higher education is leisure – the etymological meaning of the word school (*scholē* = leisure). Literally speaking, therefore, a school should be more like a place of freedom and enlightenment rather than like an efficient factory. After all, higher education is akin to liberation and awakening, rather than to training. In contrast, much of the present day post-secondary education is focused on assembly-line training, research techniques, and a fast-paced curriculum – all of which are antithetical to the very meaning of 'school' as a place of leisure meant to provide the time and place for a community of scholars to realize that an unexamined life is not worth living, and to promote a life-long interest in the examined life through reading and reflection.

Designating the promotion of the examined life as the proper end of higher education justifies its use as the primary principle for organizing the academic curriculum around a broad program of liberal studies. With such an end in view, the knowledge most worth having needs to be based on long and thoughtful reflection on the great works and the pivotal ideas in philosophy, science, religion, and literature which have engaged and exercised the greatest minds in the history of humanity, and on a critical examination of the bearing that these ideas and their modern versions have on the problems facing us in the present. Without such a foundational program of liberal studies, higher education can have very little meaning.

Some knowledge of the tradition of higher education in the West may be critical at this stage, both for appreciating the ideas which have shaped our views of liberal education, and for understanding some of the early developments in academe which initiated the changes in a direction that finally led to the present design and character of the university.

⌒— IV —⌒

Beginning in ancient Greece in the fourth century B.C., Plato's Academy served as a temple of intellect for close to a millenium. Since then it has figured prominently as the fountainhead of our very conception of higher education. The essence of the Academy consisted in the intellectual examination of ideas for the pursuit of truth by a community of scholars passionately engaged in critical and creative thought. The Academy was the very embodiment of Socratic inquiry aimed at promoting the examined life. Of course, Socrates continues to exercise our imagination and remains our teacher par excellence – even though he never published! In fact, he would have perished even sooner had he published, since his subversive inquiry into the idols of the marketplace would have undoubtedly proved his unAthenian activities to the senators of the time. Propitiously, pupil Plato published – posthumously, from the point of view of Socrates. The immortal *Dialogues* of Plato have remained unsurpassed philosophical treatises on the nature of wisdom, knowledge, education, goodness, love, beauty, virtue, happiness, justice and the state – so that, in the words of one modern philosopher, philosophy since then has indeed been "a series of footnotes to Plato."

Plato's philosophy of education called for a literate culture based on what was essentially a liberal arts curriculum, which required the mastery of several disciplines – from language and logic to mathematics and music. However, the pride of place in the curriculum was given to philosophical learning – the rational examination of abstract ideas, using dialectical thinking, for the development of a comprehensive philosophical mind which is characterized by a synoptic vision of the true principles of knowledge. The cultivation of intellect was, therefore, a necessary condition for the pursuit of theoretical truth and wisdom, so that philosophy became the centerpiece in Plato's republic of higher learning.

The enduring nature of the ancient legacy is evident from the fact that even some of the greatest minds in modern science have returned to it from time to time for intellectual sustenance and inspiration. Without a proper study of Greek thought, Socratic and pre-Socratic, education cannot claim to be 'higher' in any meaningful sense of the word. No wonder the great Goethe enjoined us to "Study Moliére, study Shakespeare, but above all study the ancient Greeks, ever and always the Greeks."[8]

The rise of the medieval universities in Italy, France and England during the twelfth and thirteenth centuries followed the revival of learning when the knowledge of Greek philosophy, science, medicine, mathematics and Roman law was brought to Western Europe by the Arab scholars in Spain. These early universities were the work of masters and students who formed a community of scholars – academic guilds, which are the origin of the word university. Happily, at first these universities had no administration to bother them, nor a board of governors to haggle with for salaries – in other words, it was as ideal a condition for the process of higher education and scholarly work as one could ask for. Unhappily, then as now, some committees of masters did have a nuisance value – although academic freedom today permits quite a bit of intellectual liberty and leeway to deal with unscrupulous administrators, colleagues, and committees.

The medieval universities introduced the professional study of medicine, law and theology in addition to the liberal arts which had already received their finest exposition both in Plato's Academy and in Aristotle's Lyceum. However, it is only in practice, not in spirit, that the medieval university shares the professional orientation with our modern universities. In stark contrast to the willy-nilly introduction of a variety of professionally oriented courses today, the curriculum of the medieval universities was based on a sound rationale. The liberal arts for the cultivation of the mind, medicine for the care of the body, law for the conduct of the individual in society, and theology for the salvation of the soul. Since medicine and law have now become lucrative professions in the West, their extrinsic value has come to outweigh their intrinsic worth in most cases. On the other hand, theology does not even occupy a prominent place in the modern universities – which, instead of saving souls, have "impoverished the souls of today's students", to repeat the terse expression of Allan Bloom.

Nevertheless, in one way, these medieval universities were different from their earlier Greek prototypes, but similar to their modern counterparts. Unlike the Academy and the Lyceum, they awarded degrees certifying the branch of learning – Bachelor's and Master's of Arts, or Doctorates in Medicine, Law and Theology. In another way, these medieval universities were similar to the early Greek institutions, but different from their modern versions. The medieval university consisted not only of a society of masters and scholars who would "gladly learn and gladly teach" à la Chaucer's Oxford clerk, but of those who were also men of general learning – even in the case of the practitioners who applied their intellectual abilities to the learned professions. Higher learning was considered to be sacred in the medieval university, not simply useful or practical as in the case of our more pragmatic universities today.

Such masters, scholars and practitioners, well versed in classical and general humanistic learning, continued through the Renaissance, and survived through the nineteenth century, even after the proposal by Wilhelm von Humboldt (1767-1835)[9] for a research based organization of institutions of higher learning had gained a foothold in some parts of Europe and in North America. Doctrates in Philosophy began to be awarded for specialized scholarship in any one of the several branches of learning. However, many of these scholars of the nineteenth century, with doctrates in Philosophy, were people of broad learning in the tradition of the seventeenth, eighteenth and earlier centuries.

With the progress of science through the nineteenth century, the need for specialized scholarship and research became quite inevitable and was firmly established in some of the major institutions of higher learning on both sides of the Atlantic. The most adverse long-term consequence of this was the fragmentation of knowledge, followed by the decline of liberal education. A somewhat different result may have ensued from a more judicious application of Humboldt's proposal for the organization of institutions of higher learning.

Humboldt's exalted view of institutions of higher learning as crowning "the moral culture of the nation" rested on the idea that "the function of such institutions lies in the development of learning (*Wissenschaft*) in its *deepest* and *broadest* sense" for "its own sake" (emphasis added). The institutions simply embodied "the spiritual life of those men drawn, by external necessity or inner élan, toward learning and research." External necessity or leisure combined with internal drive or pressures have indeed been the major conditions for learning and scholarship. Amusingly, however, under the modern publish-or-perish philosophy, the pressure has become external and the necessity internal! While conformity to such a philosophy has led to the survival of many researchers, it has contributed quite significantly to the degradation of genuine scholarship – which Humboldt viewed as learning in "its deepest and broadest sense."

Humboldt himself was a man of broad and deep learning and recognized the need for a bicameral institution consisting of a university and an academy, with some shared membership and mutual scholarly interaction. The university was to "assume practical responsibility for the guidance of young people" through teaching and scholarship, while the academy would concern itself "purely with learning" effectively serving "those observational and experimental sciences that require the rapid communication of isolated facts." By instituting this academic function of research, and adopting Helmholtz's model of each researcher adding a few bricks to the edifice of knowledge, universities contributed to a rapid accumulation of such isolated facts. The consequent development of specialisms endangered the integration of knowledge, and this cast a long shadow on the tradition of liberal education on both sides of the Atlantic. Such an increase in specialisms within academic institutions has undoubtedly contributed heavily to the eventual decline and fall of liberal education in the institutions of higher learning.

⌒— V —⌒

While the first half of the nineteenth century saw Humboldt's proposal for a university as a place for the advancement of learning, the second half of the same century witnessed a proposal by John Henry Newman (1801-1890) for the university as "a place for teaching universal knowledge."[10] However, Newman's idea of a university as a center of liberal education became badly blurred by the very advancement of learning which he had explicitly excluded from his ideal of the university. Going beyond Humboldt, Newman recommended a stronger division of intellectual labour between academies and universities because he believed that "to discover and to teach are distinct functions" and "distinct gifts" that are "not commonly found united in the same person."

While at first Newman regarded the university as being concerned only with teaching and education, not research, the march of scientific progress did not allow him to maintain such a clear-cut separation for long, so that research finally came to be included in his idea of the university. However, had Newman foreseen the forthcoming proliferation of academic and scientific specialties, he may have decided to retain his earlier distinction of functions between academies and universities – with the former dedicated to doing research specifically for the advancement of knowledge, and the latter dedicated primarily to teaching and the cultivation of the intellect. They would share in common the recognition of the primacy of scholarly inquiry and the pursuit of knowledge for its own sake. Under the present organization of universities, such a division of labor needs to be maintained between graduate training for research and undergraduate liberal education primarily for the cultivation of intellect.

As Newman saw it, liberal education serves the purpose of cultivating the intellect by the exercise of reason and reflection, which provides "a connected view of old and new, past and present, far and near ... without which there is no whole, and no centre." The resulting "enlargement of the mind" is no more than this "power of viewing many things at once as one whole" and understanding their mutual relations and significance. The cultivation of such a philosophic habit of mind through liberal education leads to the kind of "comprehensiveness and versatility of intellect" which permits a good grasp of things in general and thereby to general human learning, that the Greeks called *paidea*, and we call the humanities – which, in the traditional sense, include all the sciences and mathematics, along with philosophy, history, literature and the fine arts.

The "cultivation of intellect" for "intellectual excellence" is the sole purpose of liberal education; this is what distinguishes liberal education from technical, commercial and professional training requiring diverse mental skills. The purpose of a university, for Newman, is "not learning or acquirement" but rather "thought or reason exercised upon knowledge." The university, he believed, has done its work when "it educates the intellect to reason well in all matters, to reach out towards truth, and to grasp it." In other words, the university should be no more and no less than the fountainhead of intellectual culture.

While Oxford and Cambridge retained the classical tradition of liberal education, major universities in Germany had organized themselves as research based institutions dedicated to the advancement of learning. However, it was the classical model that was imported to New England when Harvard College was established in early seventeenth century as the first major institution of higher education with a modest liberal studies program. Many of the other colleges which followed later were seminaries of a vocational kind providing theological or teacher training. Only during the nineteenth century did they gradually expand their curriculum in pursuit of disinterested higher learning. Meanwhile, Harvard moved in the direction of professionalization, adding Medicine in the later part of the eighteenth century, followed by Divinity and Law in early nineteenth century, and the Graduate School of Arts and Science in the late nineteenth century. With the emphasis on professional training, practical education for careers, and a public service orientation to education, Harvard University offered its own unique model – made in America. With the introduction of the elective system to cater to the individual tastes and interests of students, liberal education in America essentially went under receivership. Some dedicated attempts were made to revive various versions of it during the first half of the present century at Harvard, Columbia and Chicago – which provided the three basic models of a general liberal education, adopted with modifications by many American colleges. Eventually, however, it was the elective system, in combination with a smorgasbord curriculum, which shaped the American university system into the likeness of a cafeteria in a fancy department store.

Not very long after the British model had found itself in competition with the American professional, practical and public service orientation, the German model crossed the Atlantic and established itself at the new Johns Hopkins University. Harvard, Yale and other major universities soon joined Gottingen-in-Baltimore, as Johns Hopkins was called. It was as if an American Declaration of Higher Education was ratified – giving scholars the inalienable rights to a life of academic liberty and the pursuit of a specialized Ph.D. The Ph.D. Octopus, as William James called it, gradually spread its tentacles across the North American continent – squirting ink on countless theses, while squeezing the life out of liberal education.

Thus the British, German and the American models became the nineteenth century legacy to twentieth century American education – consisting of that unique mixture of teaching, research and a service orientation which has continued to burden the North American professor with the impossible job of teaching and compulsive committee/ community service under a cut-throat publish-or-perish sword of Damocles.

The new Graduate Schools absorbed the functions that Newman had proposed for an academy by stacking graduate training on top of undergraduate education. This created the understandable illusion that research culminating in a doctorate was the very pinnacle of higher education – when all that a Ph.D. often represented was a most absurd and extreme form of specialization. The erosion of liberal education started in earnest as more and more of the indoctrinated doctorates manned the institutions of higher learning and prepared even their undergraduates to be research fodder for the graduate school labor market. This trend continued to climb as more and more undergraduate eyes lifted up from the groves of liberal colleges and gazed starry-eyed at the university ideal of graduate training.

While research and professional training characterized only the universities, even many undergraduate colleges did not hesitate to masquerade as universities, and to award honorary doctorates to celebrities – not being in a position to award them for equally ephemeral specialties. As Orwell had said of political language, academic institutions, too, were simply trying to give "the appearance of solidity to pure wind." In this confusion of tongues, the meaning and purpose of liberal education and higher learning received an inevitable setback.

Fortunately, in the first half of the present century, higher learning in America came under a searching examination from two homegrown critics within the system. Ironically, neither favored the existing homegrown model of the university, with its unique orientation which included the professional, vocational and public service components. However, each subscribed to a different vision of the ideal university.

∿— VI —∿

The vision of higher learning in America proposed by Thorstein Veblen (1857-1929) has a definite affinity with the German model of higher learning, with its emphasis on the advancement of knowledge as the primary purpose of the university. In his critique of American education, Veblen charged that the universities had become subservient to business norms, and needlessly competitive in their search for students and endowments. In thus pursuing pecuniary gains and catering to market demands, universities had shifted away from their proper ends of science and scholarship towards more professional and vocational goals. For Veblen, such a shift towards utilitarian ends was a perversion of higher learning, which should have nothing else as its aim except the advancement of learning through scholarly and scientific inquiry.

In Veblen's view, the sole function of a university is to "conserve and extend the domain of knowledge."[11] While in its function the university was to be like Humboldt's institution for the advancement of learning, in its composition Veblen's proposal had much in common with the early medieval universities. As a seminary of higher learning, a university was to be a self-governing community of scholars — with professors and students, but without presidents or governing boards – whose offices, Veblen believed, should be abolished for the "rehabilitation of learning." In the shelter of such an institution, "scholars might pursue their several lines of adventure, in teaching and inquiry" – undisturbed by routine administrative memos and meetings.

Under such circumstances, university teaching for Veblen was "subsidiary and incidental to the work of inquiry" serving only to equip and draw students into such work. Teaching is "distinctly advantageous to the investigator" since it facilitates his own work of inquiry – as modern professors with their research assistants know only too well. However, the same generalization hardly holds the other way, especially in the case of undergraduate education, where specialized research has become a definite liability for teaching in broad-based liberal studies programs. An indiscriminate publish-or-perish policy has certainly a lot to answer for in the decline of professorial interest in liberal education in the modern university.

Of course, Veblen based his case for the mutually beneficial relationship of "apprentice" with "master" on two assumptions. First, that a native gift of "idle curiosity" actuates human beings to "instinctively seek knowledge, and value it." Second, that students come to the university with "interest" and "initiative" for "the pursuit of knowledge" and to make themselves scholars in the image of their masters. While it is easy to agree with the first assumption that all human beings "desire to know," as Aristotle put it, the second assumption seems to be rather unrealistic today and holds true for not more than a small percentage of students, even in graduate schools. For most students, getting post-secondary education and training has become either a practical necessity for the job market, or one viable way of surviving periodic economic recessions – both eminently understandable reasons in a society that places more value on marketable training than on 'impractical' liberal education. Thus both professional careerism and the vocational orientation, which Veblen had decried, have become the dominant forces in the modern university.

It was this very concern, namely, that higher learning may become so adulterated by the utilitarian ethos, which had led Veblen to propose a separation of the graduate school/university from both the professional school and the undergraduate college. In fact, Veblen realized that the only reason for the coexistence of the graduate and the undergraduate departments in the same institution was the historical accident that the older American universities had grown on the ground of an underlying college, so that the holding together of these two disparate schools had been "a freak of aimless survival."

However, in the threefold scheme of Veblen, an undergraduate college was to be an institution designed to provide the incoming generation a "rounded discipline" for civil life, or "concluding touches" to those who had no designs for higher learning – although Veblen did not preclude the possibility of undergraduate colleges being preparatory to entering either a "career of learning" or the professions. On the other hand, the university was to be a center for higher learning designed exclusively for graduate students, for the pursuit of "a life of science and scholarship" and for the "increase and the diffusion of learning." Given this exclusive mandate for the university, professional schools, too, had no place in Veblen's university since they essentially served utilitarian ends – professional and technical training for jobs and careers.

According to Veblen, the formal incorporation of undergraduate, graduate and professional programs into one single academic body has adverse effects on higher learning. While he realized that the work done in professional and technological schools can be of value to university scholars, the inclusion of professionals and technologists among the academic staff empowers them to participate in shaping academic policies and the general direction of academic affairs away from the disinterested pursuit of science and scholarship, and towards utilitarian ends – albeit with "a degree of pedantry and sophistication" bordering on the "vulgar" – regardless of how successfully professional and technical schools manage to stage their "make-believe scholarship."

Ironically, Veblen's call for an absolute separation between a university and a professional school, in the interest of keeping the purity of higher learning, was lost in the ethos of a commercial culture. Subsequent developments not only proved to be contrary to Veblen's prescription, but also to his prediction. Less than half way through the present century, the utilitarian drift permanently diverted the universities to the "service of Mammon" so that higher learning became secondary to higher earnings. Yet, even if this hindered the advancement of learning, as Veblen claimed it would, nobody seemed to mind, since such a state of affairs actually enhanced the social status of universities. Veblen's ideal of free "irresponsible science and scholarship" pursued purely out of "idle curiosity" did not have a chance to flourish in a utilitarian society which saw a university only as a commercially useful commodity. Paradoxically, however, in becoming utilitarian, science also became irresponsible in a disturbing sense, while disinterested scholarship became dominated by self-promoting research, with idle curiosity contributing to much pedantic triviality.

Veblen misread the future even more in his justification for the separation of a university, with its graduate school and the disinterested pursuit of learning, from a college of undergraduate studies with a curriculum which involved "task work" and "standardized routine" methods of training and testing. The incorporation of college and university into one academic body, Veblen feared, would lead to "a gradual insinuation of undergraduate methods and standards in the graduate school" making university work into "nothing more than an extension of the undergraduate curriculum." It is obvious that Veblen's position on the separation of college and university was based on his rather lop-sided view that undergraduate work in college is necessarily training and task work, while the "work of learning" is the monopoly of the graduate school/university. Ironically, Veblen's proposed division of functions has led to a rather amusing reverse fulfillment of both his fears and his predictions. The so-called training and task work reserved for undergraduate colleges have been extended to graduate work for the advancement of learning in the university, while the specialized graduate curriculum has been extended into undergraduate work. Consequently, many undergraduate departments have turned into mini-graduate departments which serve as ideal breeding grounds for the training of the much needed research assistants who facilitate both the advancement of learning and the careers of their mentors – thus contributing to the explosion of information and the inflation of academic egos.

While focusing on the need for three distinct institutions, with the university reserved only for the advancement and diffusion of learning, Veblen bypassed the whole issue of the place of liberal education in his critical assessment of higher learning. One would have expected that he would have explicitly provided for liberal education at the undergraduate college level to assure the extension of an educated frame of mind to the work of disinterested scholarship and the advancement of learning in the university. Unfortunately, in Veblen's scheme, learning and scholarship were left idling with mere curiosity.

Fortunately, however, less than two decades after Veblen's incisive analysis of the American university system, higher learning in America was once again subjected to a critique – but this time it was from the vantage point of making liberal education the foundation of higher learning.

✐— VII —✎

According to Robert Maynard Hutchins (1899-1977), president of the University of Chicago (1929-1945), there were two ways to make a great university – either by having a great football team or a great president. Too much emphasis on sports and social life, he believed, had contributed more than a fair share to the debasement of higher learning in America. Ergo, the University's football team was duly disbanded, and Hutchins went on to tackle the confusion that beset American colleges and universities by championing the goal of universal liberal education.

Some of the causes of academic confusion that Hutchins identified more than half a century ago are still very much in operation. The "service-station conception of a university" that continues to dominate the modern university has resulted from the "love of money" and the consequent "sensitivity to public demands" which it requires to obtain or maintain the financing from students, donors or governments. "It is sad but true," said Hutchins, "that when an institution determines to do something in order to get the money it must lose its soul, and frequently does not get the money."[12] Such a story has repeated itself quite often over the years, but the captains of the knowledge industry have continued to allow their educational policies to be dictated by the accidents of fads and funding – thus allowing the soul of a university to be dismembered and sold in bits and pieces to the highest bidders of the private and public marts.

The sensitivity of a university to public opinion and market demands seems to follow from a utilitarian conception of higher learning in which the prime object of education is economic – better jobs and higher wages. It is obvious that when education is seen only as a way of getting more money, the universities get degraded into vocational schools.

For the university, too, the love of money may be the root of some evils. Finding the infinite proliferation of courses repulsive, Hutchins noted that "the educational system as a whole needs *less money* rather than more" (emphasis added) – if a university does not try to be all things to all people. In fact, he argued that "a reduction of its income would force it to reconsider its expenditures" on "activities that ought to be abandoned." Hutchins rightly attributed such disgraceful waste on "extravagant enterprises" to the "self-interest of professors" and the "vanity of administrators" with which we have all become familiar over the years, as professors and presidents periodically propose policies and programs purely for purposes of power, prestige and personal gain.

Thus, Hutchins did not believe that the decline in liberal education programs could be attributed to lack of funds – especially not in the humanities and social studies. However, he realized that the scientific ethos had led many scholars in these fields to "dedicate themselves to the aimless accumulation of data about trivial subjects" – albeit under serious misconceptions about the scientific method and scientific progress.

The tenacious hold that the doctrine of progress has on the modern temper is the consequence of the striking advances that have occurred in science and technology. Since the many discoveries and inventions seemed to result from the application of the empirical method of science in the accumulation of data, it was easy to make the facile generalization that obtaining more information would lead to similar progress even in the more humane disciplines. Thus the empirical method became identified with progress in knowledge and, as Hutchins realized, "empiricism, having taken the place of thought as the basis of research, took its place, too, as the basis of education" and "led by easy stages to vocationalism." Education thus became a matter of learning useful facts which make for the best adaptation to the occupational environment.

Despite claims to the contrary, many modern universities are heavily imbued with both vocationalism and professionalism – jobs and careers. In such a utilitarian context, it appears almost ridiculous to believe in, or to talk about, the cultivation of intellect for its own sake. "Thus the modern temper," concludes Hutchins, "produces that strangest of modern phenomena, an anti-intellectual university." In such a university, ability in critical thinking or interest in ideas can even be a handicap for the careers of both the professor and the pupil.

What is higher learning for Hutchins? "As education it is the single-minded pursuit of intellectual virtues. As scholarship it is the single-minded devotion to the advancement of knowledge." For Hutchins, modern education would not qualify as higher learning – since it is blatantly utilitarian and anti-intellectual; nor would much of present day research qualify as scholarship – since it involves the aimless accumulation of unnecessary data, isolated facts and trivial information, which hardly lead to a proportionate advancement of knowledge.

According to Hutchins, such a state of affairs in universities had resulted from confusing science with information, ideas with facts and knowledge with data. The utilitarian emphasis in education, combined with a blind empiricism in research, had degraded both education and scholarship to a point which led Hutchins to fear that the "pursuit of knowledge for its own sake [was] being rapidly obscured in universities and may soon be extinguished."

The rise of new academic programs catering to a variety of professions and specialisms – from business, journalism, public administration, and social work to nursing and pharmacy, changed the character and composition of the university in the twentieth century. These new developments inevitably led to further dilemmas and divisiveness in the world of higher learning. However, Hutchins did not decry the fact of universities adding on professional programs as such, as Veblen had done. In fact, Hutchins believed that without such an association with universities which serve as "centers of creative thought" providing an intellectual emphasis on ideas, theory and principles, professional schools degenerate into trade schools, dealing merely with practical problems, techniques and tricks of the trade. It was obvious to him that "turning professional schools into vocational schools degrades the universities, and does not elevate the professions." Students may therefore enter a learned profession well-trained in practice, but without having been properly educated in the intellectual aspects of the discipline. Unfortunately, such non-intellectual vocationalism of the professions today makes it difficult to regard even law and medicine as 'learned' professions, as was the case in the past. It almost seems as if in becoming lucrative, these respectable professions also became less learned.

The vocationalization of the university also leads to the trivialization of the whole academic curriculum, and a debasement of the university as "a haven where the search for truth may go on unhampered by utility or pressure for 'results'." The professional atmosphere today has become so all pervasive in universities that even the non-professional departments of arts and sciences have become utilitarian, as Veblen had feared. Here then is the dilemma of professionalism: since the subject matter of the learned professions is intellectual, in principle professional programs belong in the university; yet, in practice, the vocational emphasis in such programs today ends up dominating the whole educational atmosphere of the university – which nullifies the value of incorporating professional programs in a university.

Professionalism with a vocational emphasis gives rise to specialisms which, in turn, create a fragmentation of the university into isolated disciplines. Time-consuming professional and specialist studies become divorced from the common body of basic knowledge that is so essential a part of good education. Hutchins was therefore rightly concerned that the demand on the part of the professions, the public and the government for specialized training for jobs and careers subverts "the unifying principle of a university [which] is the pursuit of truth for its own sake."

The only solution that Hutchins saw for the blight of professionalism, specialism and anti-intellectualism eroding the institutions of higher learning was the development of "general education" – with all advanced study resting on a common body of knowledge. Such a unified intellectual base, he believed, was necessary for making our universities "true communities and communities of true scholars." For Hutchins, the real justification for the special privileges of universities reside, not in their being social clubs for the affluent or vocational institutions for the rest, but in the "enduring value of having constantly before our eyes institutions that represent an abiding faith in the highest powers of mankind."

Such faith can only be promoted when professors and students share a common intellectual training and "a common stock of fundamental ideas." However, the overemphasis on empiricism, with the consequent explosion of specialized information, has not only undermined the rational emphasis on such fundamental ideas, but has also forced out general education and the liberal arts from the academic curriculum. The insidious splitting of most disciplines into multiple specialisms has thus had extremely adverse effects on communication and mutual understanding between members of different disciplines and specialties.

For Hutchins, education is rightly understood only as the cultivation of intellect, which is a good worth pursuing for its own sake – as well as for its inestimable value both in a life of contemplation and in a life of action. Logically speaking, education implies teaching, which implies knowledge, which implies the existence of truth, which has to be the same for all; hence, concludes Hutchins, "education should everywhere be the same." Moreover, he notes, " one purpose of education is to draw out the elements of our common human nature" and these are "the same in any time or place" for everyone. Hence he concludes that the idea of education for the purpose of adjusting students to live in particular environments is "foreign to a true conception of education."

To draw out the elements of our common human nature, Hutchins proposed a coherent and comprehensive curriculum composed of what he called the "permanent studies" – studies which connect human beings together, connect us to our intellectual heritage, connect the past with the present, and connect us to the best that has been thought and said in the world. Being the foundation of all academic disciplines, the permanent studies should be at the heart of higher education. For only through such studies, which emphasize the ideational basis of our current knowledge, can one gain entry into the intellectual culture of humanity, and comprehend the ideas at work in the contemporary world.

For Hutchins, a general education curriculum of permanent studies consisted of two parts: a study of the great books of the Western world which literally cover every department of knowledge, and a study of grammar, rhetoric, logic and mathematics which provided mastery of the liberal arts of reading, writing, speaking, thinking and reasoning. Hutchins believed that we cannot call someone educated if they have never read any of the great books – classics of philosophy, science and literature which are contemporary and comprehensible in every age. He was convinced that "the confusion of modern thought and the modern world resulted from the loss of what has been thought and done in earlier ages."

A liberal arts curriculum which includes the works of the great liberal artists provides the ideal kind of general education. It not only serves as the best preparation for those who wish to pursue advanced or specialized studies, but enables all to share in the intellectual culture by raising the general standards of taste and thought. Such a curriculum, Hutchins believed, would satisfy the needs for general education in our universities.

However, even such an intellectually sound curriculum could not take root in universities which, as Hutchins noted, had become organized like encyclopedias – in alphabetical arrangement of departments from art and biology to veterinary science and zoology – without any rational unity. "Why is it that the chief characteristic of higher learning is disorder?" Hutchins asked. "It is because there is no ordering principle in it" he answered. In the Greek Academy, all thought was unified by metaphysics which, as the study of first principles, stood at the apex of an hierarchy of truths from the significant to the subsidiary. In the medieval universities, theology replaced metaphysics as the ordering principle, and the academic emphasis shifted to the study of truths about God's relations with human beings and the world of nature.

The modern university has no such ordering principle and is disordered by the anti-intellectual elements of vocationalism and empiricism – with an overemphasis on jobs and careers, and an overload of trivial information and undigested data. However, Hutchins did not deride either empirical research or professional training, but he did believe that they belonged properly in research and technical institutes attached to universities, but not within the university faculties. Such institutes, Hutchins believed, would "draw off the empiricism and vocationalism that have been strangling the universities" and "leave them free to do their intellectual job."

According to Hutchins, "higher learning is concerned primarily with thinking about fundamental problems." Research required for the progress of the sciences must follow such education – a suggestion that needs to be taken seriously if we are to save our undergraduate programs from the intellectually blind empiricism that is so widely prevalent in our universities today. Such obstacles to higher learning may be removed if, as Hutchins says, we allow only members of the faculties involved in teaching and thinking about fundamental ideas and intellectual problems to conduct the affairs of the university. It would seem to follow from the Hutchins plan that bureaucratic administrators with little time or energy for intellectual interests would, ipso facto, be left out of decision-making with regard to academic matters. Universities would thereby come close to the ideal of self-governing communities of scholars engaged in an intellectually oriented education which presents the world of thought as "a comprehensible whole."

Hutchins was convinced that only a rational plan, such as he had proposed, would make the university "a true center of learning" and "the home of creative thought." Alas, Hutchins represented a minority voice in the academic wilderness. With some minor exceptions, even his rational vision of higher learning failed to influence the major course of events in the North American universities. On the contrary, vocationalism, professionalism, empiricism, anti-intellectualism, departmentalism and specialisms have since taken on ominous dimensions. The decline and fall of higher education in the modern university now constitutes a serious threat to the future of literacy itself.

Chapter 2

. . . .

Illiberal Education
and Intellectual Illiteracy

Literacy is threatened as much by modern education as by modern communication.

> - Ivan Illich and Barry Saunders
> *The Alphabetization of the Popular Mind*[1]

T he paradox of modern education and communication as threats to literacy would surely appear to be enigmatic to anyone who associates illiteracy only with poverty and industrial backwardness, not with affluence and scientific progress. Yet, concern about declining literacy even in the educational institutions of technologically advanced nations seems to suggest that we are dealing with a phenomenon of an unprecedented magnitude, if not with a riddle wrapped in a mystery. Why Johnny can't read well, write effectively, or think critically has puzzled, troubled and humbled many conscientious educators. Such bewilderment can be cleared up only by a critical examination of the various forms of literacy.

While the general aim of education is literacy, there seems to be some lack of clarity and consistency in the ways in which literacy has been conceived in various discussions on the subject. There is, therefore, a clear need to identify the different forms in which literacy may be said to manifest itself during the whole course of education from school to college and university. Going from the simple and specific to the more complex and general forms, it seems possible to identify at least four fairly distinct forms of literacy: *basic literacy, cultural literacy, academic literacy,* and *intellectual literacy.*

Of these forms, only *basic literacy* has a commonly understood and acceptable meaning referring to the possession of the general skills of reading, writing and reckoning. Essential as such skills are to all higher forms of literacy, it is obvious that merely being functionally literate in this sense does not imply that one is literate in the sense of being well-informed, well-read or well-educated. These latter outcomes of education, therefore, cannot be understood in terms of basic literacy, so that we need to make some meaningful distinctions between our varied educational experiences as different forms of literacy.

In a recent treatise on the subject, *cultural literacy* has been viewed as the "broadly shared background knowledge" about historical, national, social, political, literary and scientific matters. Being well-informed about cultural facts has a functional value as a basis for promoting both effective communication and essential learning. Cultural literacy therefore needs to be inculcated extensively in schools. However, the amount of such cultural information is so vast that, at best, this exercise can amount to little more than providing a veneer of education with relatively broad and decontextualized general knowledge, but no discernibly rational basis for evaluating its significance in the overall historical context of knowledge.

We cannot, therefore, stop with cultural literacy as a final educational aim, as E.D. Hirsch himself realized:

> Cultural literacy is a necessary but not sufficient attainment of an educated person. Cultural literacy is shallow; true education is deep. Because broad knowledge enables us to read and learn effectively, it is the best guarantee that we will continue to read, and learn, and deepen our knowledge. True literacy has always opened doors – not just to deep knowledge and economic success, but also to other people and other cultures.[2]

Thus, cultural literacy cannot be set up as the end of higher education even in a data-based society that worships information for its own sake. It is necessary to go both deeper and higher at the university level.

University education would only be a notch higher than programs on National Educational Television unless it offered the two indispensable forms of literacy represented by: *academic literacy* - defined in terms of knowledge, training and research in specialized scholarly disciplines; and *intellectual literacy* - defined in terms of a general education based on comprehensive and contextualized knowledge, grounded in an appreciation of a variety of historically significant and universal ideas embodied in the great creative works of human intellect and imagination. Of these two, it is intellectual literacy which legitimately constitutes the primary and proper goal of higher education based on liberal studies.

We have in these four forms of literacy all that makes for a literate culture: tools of learning, information, knowledge, and ideas. One would expect that our schools are taking care of at least the first two forms of literacy (basic and cultural), while colleges and universities are actively promoting the academic and intellectual forms of literacy. Of course, this is simply the illusion we complacently maintain even in the face of much contrary evidence that critics have brought to public attention over the last several years. While there are fine educational institutions, they are few and far between, and certainly not sufficient to contribute to any significant enhancement of a literate culture. In fact, the irony is that modern education and communication systems have actually promoted a literal culture which has become a threat to a literate culture. The cult of information has literally displaced the culture of intellect, ideas, and imagination.

Thus the very possibility of promoting an educated imagination, which is at home in the two cultures of science and humanities, has been eroded in institutions of higher learning. The forces of unbridled empiricism, professionalism and vocationalism have combined to produce what Ortega y Gasset called the "barbarism" of academic specialization[3] – which seems to have an affinity with a literal culture that is dominated by a utilitarian ethos, and is guided by blatantly commercial considerations. The mass production of disconnected information bombarding our sensibilities leaves little time or inclination for understanding the interconnectedness of knowledge.

Such a development certainly appears to be one of the great paradoxes of our century. Overwhelmed with the mass of varied and conflicting information, we seem to have become not only less well-informed and less critical, but also very confused and gullible. Even as we witness an unprecedented increase in the amount of reading material, and a phenomenal increase in book-buying, T.V. programs and internet surfing remain far ahead of book reading. Even with momentous advances in knowledge, we do not seem to have gained real understanding. Even with substantial increases in the number of students in schools, colleges and universities, society as a whole does not seem to have become significantly better educated.

Much of this may indeed be attributed to the fact that, despite the information explosion made possible by an efficient organization of the knowledge industry, the individual human capacity to absorb information, evaluate knowledge claims, judge significance, imagine consequences, and comprehend meanings has not improved to any appreciable degree. Thus the mass production of knowledge on the academic assembly-line has enlarged the domain of the knowable without enhancing the capacity of the individual knowers to comprehend the whole. In fragmenting the world of knowledge we seem to have also fragmented the minds of the knowers.

Such fragmentation due to information overload leads to a sense of alienation, and consequently to a loss of ability to comprehend the world. Since the world seems to belong to us only to the extent that we understand it as a comprehensive whole, we have no choice other than that of providing the kind of higher education which creates an overall understanding of the unity and continuity of knowledge – that is, a liberal education based on a generalist-humanist approach to all disciplines.

Higher education can be regarded as higher and humanistic only to the extent that it introduces the students to a thoughtful study of a variety of pivotal ideas which have animated human consciousness and cultures down the ages: Truth, Beauty, Goodness, Form, Nature, Harmony, Matter, Time and Space, Mind, Soul, God, Human Being, Life and Death, Eternity, Infinity, Free-Will, Determinism, Desire, Courage, Wisdom, Knowledge, Love, Pleasure, Happiness, Pain, Evil, Liberty, Equality, Morality, Law, Justice, State, Government, Citizen, Duty, Progress, Evolution, Revolution, War and Peace, Wealth, Labor and Family.[4] Without such ideas human civilization itself would be unthinkable. Thus, it is not the accumulation of general and popular information or cultural facts, but the historically grounded comprehension of such universal ideas and their significance in the human enterprise that constitutes intellectual literacy. Ideally, such general learning should be the foundation of all higher education.

The popular alternative, presently in existence, is to promote the illusion of higher education with some combination of the following: an accumulation of usually unconnected facts (cultural and/or technical), the learning of professional/vocational skills, and premature specialization which limits the scope of general understanding, but fosters an arrogance of mastery. Even academic literacy, which should mean the broad mastery of at least one discipline, has been reduced to a mockery by the multiple sub-specialisms that threaten the unity of most academic disciplines and prevent the broad mastery and understanding of even one discipline.

While the strategy of specialization has its value in higher learning, especially in the sciences and in a few other divisible disciplines, its earliest and proper place of entry in the university system would be at the graduate level, upon completion of an undergraduate program of liberal studies which foster intellectual literacy. It is clearly necessary to be civilized before we become specialized, since a humane vision is critical in protecting us from the dangers of specialist tunnel-vision.

Thus all forms of literacy have their reasons and seasons in the scheme of education. However, neither cultural literacy with its emphasis on general knowledge and cultural facts, nor academic literacy with its emphasis on specialized knowledge of various disciplines, can fulfill the humanizing aim of higher education. In fact, much of the information deemed necessary for cultural literacy may be imbibed far more efficiently from television than from an educational institution. Likewise, interactive computer programs and even distance education can reliably provide much of the specialized knowledge and training that goes with academic literacy – which basically involves acquiring specialized information, mastering the rules of research, attaining technical proficiency and solving problems that often have only disciplinary significance. Only in the case of intellectual literacy is the prime emphasis placed on a humanized setting for the cultivation of intellect through a critical discussion of the significant ideas of humanity witnessed in the best that has been thought and said in the world.

Criticism, as Matthew Arnold defined it, is "the disinterested endeavor to learn and propagate the best that is known and thought in the world."[5] Our answer as to how much of what is current in the humanities would be included in the "best that is known and thought in the world" must be the same as that of Arnold's with regard to the then current English Literature: "Not very much." As Barzun also observed: "The truth is that dealing with the contemporary prepares the mind poorly for a thoughtful life, shortening judgment and distorting perspective."[6] We can be fully humanized in this sense of developing a thoughtful life, mature judgment and broad perspective only by such a confrontation with the vast heritage of philosophical, scientific, social, political, moral and religious thought which provides a full awareness of the traditions of humanity. A truly literate culture can therefore exist only on the basis of such intellectual literacy. It is not enough to be well-informed or be well-trained to be well-educated, but it is enough to be well-educated to have a mind liberated from the prejudices of one's own time and culture.

Thus intellectual literacy can best be fostered by liberal education, not by academic specialization, however important the latter may be for the technical advancement of knowledge. Professional and vocational training for careers and jobs contribute technicians to the economy, not free and well-educated citizens. However, the order of things in a technological society favors only what is utilitarian and degrades the value of higher education by ignoring the broad horizon of humanity's intellectual tradition. Jacques Ellul captures the modern temper in his penetrating analysis of the dangers of a technological society:

> Education ... is becoming oriented toward the specialized end of producing technicians; and, as a consequence, toward the creation of individuals useful only as members of a technical group, on the basis of the current criteria of utility – individuals who conform to the structure and the needs of the technical group. The intelligentsia will no longer be a model, a conscience or an animating intellectual spirit for the group, even in the sense of performing a critical function. They will be the servants, the most conformist imaginable, of the instruments of technique. ... And education will no longer be an unpredictable and exciting adventure in human enlightenment, but an exercise in conformity and an apprenticeship to whatever gadgetry is useful in a technical world.[7]

By definition, conformity is incompatible with the critical function. Hence any kind of education that promotes critical thinking would find itself on a list of endangered species in a conformist society. It is the paradox of a technological culture that even while it frees us for leisure, it enslaves us to its own rules and rituals in a manner so benign that it is hard to notice the erosion of our critical faculties until robopathy sets in. Of course, the antidote is there in the form of intellectual literacy which promotes a comprehensive and critical understanding of the historical and philosophical context of the human predicament. All other forms of literacy – tools of learning, cultural information and specialized knowledge – are quite compatible with the ultra-utilitarian orientation and the totalitarian tendency of a technocratic society. Only intellectual literacy can serve as the bulwark against the onslaught of a mind-numbing conformity to bureaucracy and technology.

∽— II —∾

In such a technological context, it was inevitable for computer literacy to become the new kid on the literacy block, and to excite the imagination of all progressive minded parents, teachers and academic researchers. More to the point, the enthusiasm of students shifted rather easily from the television tube to the video screen monitor of the friendly neighborhood computer. Apple and IBM received accolades as user-friendly teachers for the new age of technology. However, this technological fix brought with it new problems. While more technolgically sophisticated, the computer-literate Johnny now has little interest in reading books. The gadgetry, gimmicks and games of our specialized and speeded-up culture of technology have left little time for such slow-paced activities like reading, especially the classic works of humanity that promote reflective thought and imagination. Johnny and his computermates have thus become super-surfers on the electronic superhighways, and super-efficient information-processing videots – smart, but illiterate in the traditional sense of the term.

There can be little doubt that there is an incompatibility between the universal literature of humanity based on a library of great books and the new modes of acquiring information and knowledge, as Alvin Kernan observes in his reflections on 'the death of literature':

> Literature began to lose its authority, and consequently its reality, at the same time that the ability to read the book, literacy, was decreasing, that audiovisual images, film, television, and computer screen, were replacing the printed book as the most efficient and preferred source of entertainment and knowledge. Television, computer database, Xerox, wordprocessor, tape, and VCR are not symbiotic with literature and its values in the way that print was, and new ways of acquiring, storing, and transmitting information is signaling the end of a conception of writing and reading oriented to the printed book and institutionalized as literature.[8]

Where once the television alone had consumed several thousand student hours, the demand for computer literacy now takes up any remaining time to prepare the student with the tools of adjustment to a technical/electronic environment. But it is neither the time spent nor the skill acquired which create the problem. Rather it is the redefinition of human beings in the image of the computer that constitutes the danger, since it undermines the very idea of intellectual literacy. In his critique of what he calls 'Technopoly' (by which he means totalitarian technocracy), Neil Postman underlines the danger of conceiving ourselves as thinking machines: "We have devalued the singular human capacity to see things whole in all their psychic, emotional and moral dimensions, and we have replaced this with faith in the powers of technical calculation."[9]

Armed with basic literacy, computer literacy and varying degrees of low cultural literacy, masses of students enter the portals of academic institutions – where many spend an inordinate amount of time in acquiring varying degrees of social, political, athletic and sundry skills, in addition to isolated packages of information and technical skills in fairly specialized disciplines. But this is usually through no fault or rational choice of their own. What Harold Innis had to say in this regard during the early fifties is even more true for students today:

> The university graduate is illiterate as a result of the systematic poisoning of the educational system. Students and teacher are loaded down with information and prejudice. The capacity to break down prejudice and to maintain an open mind has been seriously weakened.... The results have been a systematic closing of the students' minds.[10]

Despite perfunctory student advisement, the majority of students who come with no set goals, professions or careers in mind have a hard time steering their way through a cafeteria-style elective system which is geared to counting courses and credits. Far more credit-worthy would be a curriculum with substantive content which provides the students with an opportunity to become well-read and well-educated, so that they would be able to integrate their learning and develop a broad and comprehensive view of the intellectual and moral currents of our time.

The need for a unified conception of higher education is crucial in a centrifugal culture torn apart by those social and political agendas which eventually find their way into an academic curriculum already fragmented by disciplinary specialisms. Such diversification in the content of education not only dissipates a great deal of energy, but it destroys the very possibility of any shared experience that one expects from higher education. So we end up with the anomaly that the degree of communication and understanding between the academically trained and educated today is almost inversely related to the degree of their training and education – unless they share specialties or ideologies!

Under these circumstances, institutions of higher education have been turned into an odd mixture of academies for technical training and research, which are at the same time political camps for brandishing ideologies, old and new, left and right. Supported by a self-serving and ever expanding bureaucracy, such a development has created a new breed of educators who are busy cloning future technicians, ideologues and demogogues to run our technologically complex and politically pluralistic society. It is precisely such a state of academic affairs which makes it obvious that the educational concerns of students are taking second place to the interests, goals, agendas and demands of educators, bureaucrats, government and industry. As sociologist John R. Seeley has also observed:

> It is clear that the present university is owned by a riffraff of special interests, economic, political, administrative and intellectual. It is owned in the sense that coercive, alien and destructive decisions can be and are made by these or their representatives over the conditions and nature of the university's life.[11]

Of course, while the fault lies in these agents or agencies, not in their stars, it is not always a deliberate hoodwinking of the student and the public. In fact, if the university is perceived simply as a nationalized industry like any other, then the technical, professional and vocational currents in academic training would seem quite legitimate. The university then becomes analogous to a business corporation concerned with the production of industrial commodities. However, as an industry, the university shares the sickness of a society driven by technology – which means that it can no longer be guided by an ideal of higher education that includes a prime responsibility for raising the intellectual, moral and spiritual tenor of a nation.

❧— III —❧

It is perfectly understandable that in the context of a pluralistic, multiracial, and multicultural society, educational institutions will work towards multiple goals and objectives. By and large, modern universities, including the multiversity, seem to reflect just such a diversity. Thus the question here is not whether academic institutions should be concerned with these multifarious ends, but whether they should all be claiming to provide higher education. In view of the conceptual distinctions we have introduced earlier, it would seem appropriate to suggest that only those institutions which aim at providing intellectual literacy may claim to be concerned with higher education in the proper sense of term. In the case of institutions where the major focus is on academic literacy or professional and technical training, we are dealing with what may be more properly called post-secondary education or professional training.

Much of the confusion, mixed feelings, and contrary opinions about the proper business of academic institutions seem to stem from ignoring the question of what we take to be the ends of education. In this we act very much like the Sophists of ancient Greece who set themselves up as teachers of excellence and efficiency in living, but never tried to define what they believed to be the purpose of life – other than achieving worldly success. However, what we need to guide us here is the Socratic critique which makes excellence a function of the knowledge of ends, so that there is simply no way to talk about teaching "excellence in living" per se, without knowledge of the proper end of life. The moral is clear: education, like excellence, can be meaningfully defined only in light of the ends pursued.

Applying the Socratic approach we can also see that unless we clearly specify educational ends we cannot talk meaningfully about excellence in learning. Obviously, the pursuit of excellence in the context of a university has to do, first and foremost, with the cultivation of the mind through intellectual literacy which is made possible by liberal education.

It should be clear that we are not acting like Humpty Dumpty and using words to mean just what we choose to mean. In fact, like Alice, we have asked the question whether one can make words mean different things. In the case of higher education, there seems to be no other choice – given the fact that we can make reasonable distinctions between different forms of literacy, and the fact that the majority of academic institutions cater to the intellectual variety of literacy at a hardly recognizable level, or not at all. Without intellectual literacy, an educational institution can be no higher than a polytechnic, trade or professional school – all of which provide technical and specialized training for jobs and careers.

What is in question here is not the quality of education, but the kind of education: higher education, liberal studies and intellectual literacy forming one coherent alternative; whereas post-secondary education, useful or discipline oriented studies/research, and academic literacy and/or professional competency forming another consistent alternative. Of course, it would be ideal to have a balanced combination of both the liberal and useful studies in a unified curriculum at the undergraduate level – a package which many universities claim to offer. However, given the present trends in academic institutions, the liberal and useful cannot be combined without the useful driving out the liberal – just as bad money drives out the good money, as per Gresham's law.

Semantics aside, the diversity of institutional goals and objectives is a fact of life in academia. Curricular uniformity, especially in the case of liberal studies, at any level of academic education receives scant support from either the technocratic-cum-bureaucratic administrators or the career-minded faculty and students. Add to these the equally formidable forces of a market value orientation, politically correct thinking, and post-modernist interests, and we have as hopeless a situation as could be imagined for working out anything remotely resembling a curriculum with a unified purpose – which would provide an experience of a shared intellectual tradition to all who pass through the portals of our colleges and universities. Without such a foundation of intellectual uniformity in the welter of academic diversity, we can only march up the tower of Babel.

Thus, partly from pedantic arrogance, and partly from academic astigmatism, the ivory tower, too, has been beset by what seems like an irreversible confusion of tongues. In such a climate of opinion, the dream of universal liberal education for promoting intellectual excellence seems like a relic of a reactionary past, dear only to the hearts of the technologically unsophisticated, ethnically uninformed and the politically inept. Thus, according to the new ideology, even the so-called great works in the Western canon are no more than outmoded forms of thought, of mostly male authors, whose context of discourse was Eurocentric – a limitation which has supposedly been transcended by more enlightened perspectives. However, despite seemingly serious built-in biases, a liberal education curriculum can still claim to incorporate a sense of universality which is abrogated in the exclusionary perspectives based on race, ethnic and gender differences.

Yet, given the diversity of educational agendas and the assortment of competing interests, it may seem a bit out of step to suggest that a higher education which provides intellectual literacy should form an absolute requirement for all academic education – ideal as such a state of affairs would be for broadening the horizon of those who will later proceed to get professional, vocational and technical training. Perhaps this is also a bit much to expect since, under the strain of a high information overload, a literal culture has fragmented a literate culture into a cacophony of specialized interest groups within and without academic institutions.

A specialized discipline-oriented university is inimical to liberal education and to intellectual literacy. So is mass education. Both, however, are quite hospitable to technocracy, bureaucracy and the politics of expediency. Waving the flag of progress, the learned administrative experts with red tape have almost gagged critical thinking itself out of academic existence, even as they have unthinkingly extended the red carpet to their political and industrial masters – who pay these administrative pipers and call the academic tune. Of all the forms of literacy, only intellectual literacy constitutes a serious threat to the status quo of the entrenched technocracy, bureaucracy and other political vulgarities of our specialized and collectivist society. Hence the present unpopularity of liberal education which values intellectual literacy and autonomy above technical utility, efficiency, productivity and political gimmickry.

◠— IV —◡

Since liberal education is education which is fostered by leisure, and is also education for leisure, no longer for a governing elite, it faces a serious obstacle in an affluent society. Commenting on the immense complexity of modern industrial society and the enormous claims it makes on our time and attention, E.F. Schumacher observed that "in spite of an incredible proliferation of labor saving devices," modern industrial society "has not given people more time to devote to their all-important spiritual tasks." Paradoxical as it may seem, he noted, "the amount of genuine leisure available in a society is generally in inverse proportion to the amount of labor-saving machinery it employs."[12] In such a society leisure itself becomes just another commercialized industry with numerous diversions competing with each other for the consumer's time, energy and money. Everybody wants to get on the hurry-wagon to fill up the vacant time with whatever technological tinker-toys provide a quick escape from the routine of humdrum work like reading and reflection.

Not only is a context of hurried leisure totally at odds with education, but it is unfavorable even to the poetic dimension of human life which has given rise to some of the greatest works of imaginative literature that are an intrinsic part of liberal education. What Oscar Wilde had noted in his personal impressions of America during the late nineteenth century is still an apt summary of the plight of our leisured society: "Had Romeo or Juliet been in a constant state of anxiety about trains [or planes], or had their minds been agitated by the question of return tickets, Shakespeare could not have given us those lovely balcony scenes which are so full of poetry and pathos."[13]

As much as leisure is a necessary condition for liberal education, so too is a non-utilitarian context where intrinsic ends are valued more than extrinsic goals, and cultivation of the mind is valued for its own sake. Such a radical shift in values seems like an almost unattainable ideal for a society in which the job market has no place for individuals who are simply well-educated, but does have lucrative jobs only for those who are well-trained technicians or specialists of one sort or another. It is therefore difficult to find a favorable reception for liberal education in a technical society, which has little use for the general education of its citizens – unless they possess marketable skills adaptable to some narrow sector of our vast industrial state.

Modern industrial society thus makes a heavy demand for the kind of professional, technical and vocational training which is now the centerpiece of modern post-secondary education. With appropriate use of modern electronic video and computer technology, it has become easy for academic institutions to inform and train masses of students efficiently and effectively for jobs and careers in a variety of sectors. However necessary such educational factories may be for the smooth fitting of human cogs into the industrial machine, they are simply incapable of catering to intellectual literacy which enables us to reflect critically on the human condition even in such a technological society. Thus, mass production of goods can have no educational counterpart in any meaningful sense of the term – if such critical understanding is the central concern of higher education. What is called mass education is only mass training for the transmission of information and skills to the masses; it is clearly not education geared to intellectual literacy based on reflective thought.

Thus, several developments in society, technology and education seem to have contributed to the rise in intellectual illiteracy: a conformist society, a technical environment, mass education, bureaucratization, specialization, and a market orientation. As a result, the necessary critical distance between academy and society has not simply diminished, it has virtually disappeared. Of course, there is method in such academic madness. The very survival and prosperity of academic institutions required the accommodation of educational values to the pecuniary values of a highly industrialized business culture. Such vulgarization of education, reinforced by a specialized technical superstructure, could have had no consequence other than the devaluation of intellectual literacy in present-day education.

The modern university has thus become so entangled with extraneous forces that it has become cut off from the intellectual and moral currents which had served as its élan vital. The apathy and indifference that overtake even some of the brightest students entering university may be traced to the assembly-line education which processes students like so much raw data to be fitted somewhere on the curve of employment in the scheme of the national economy. The use of the business criterion of cost-effectiveness for educational programs reflects a bureaucratic mentality truncated by technological tomfoolery. Moreover, such vulgarization of higher education also degrades the intellectual and moral qualities which have become so critical in dealing with those very conditions that are responsible for their degradation in the first place.

The corruption of intellectual literacy in our utilitarian universities is obviously a function of the displacement of liberal studies by specialist and vocational training. Such a shift seems to be associated inevitably with the need for public and government support of academic institutions, as Richard Weaver noted in his incisive comments on the utilitarian sell-out of universities:

> Nothing is more certain than that whatever has to court public favor
> for its support will sooner or later be prostituted to utilitarian ends.
> The educational institutions of the United States afford a striking
> demonstration of this truth. Virtually without exception, liberal

education, that is to say, education centered about ideas and ideals, has fared best in those institutions which draw their income from private sources. They have been able, despite limitations donors have sought to lay upon them, to insist that education be not entirely a means of breadwinning. This means that they have been relatively free to promote pure knowledge and the training of the mind; they have afforded a last stand for "antisocial" studies like Latin and Greek. In state institutions, always at the mercy of elected bodies and of the public generally, and under obligation to show practical fruits for their expenditure of money, the movement toward specialism and vocationalism has been irresistible. They have never been able to say that they will do what they will with their own because their own is not private. It seems fair to say that the opposite of the private is the prostitute.[14]

During the forty-plus years since that trend was noted, most universities have literally auctioned the academic curriculum to the vocational and technical demands of government and industry, while both public and private funding agencies have turned academics into "call girls"[15] – to use Arthur Koestler's laconic expression for those distinguished academics who organize much of their professional time soliciting the favors of the public and private moneylenders for their esoteric congresses.

∾ V ∾

With the greater demand for academic training, a larger portion of funding from business, industry and government has been funneled into research and development – the catchwords that ring so loudly in the many hallowed halls of academe. As a result, relatively less remains available for smaller institutions that are trying to offer undergraduate liberal education programs. A commercialized conception of a university as a knowledge industry inevitably causes a shift in the values that govern the institutions of higher education. Even as a growth orientation in academia has led to successes in materialistic terms, the universities at the same time seem to have become centers of spiritual decay. Commenting on the risks of success, James A. Perkins astutely observed:

> The modern university is one of those strange paradoxes of human affairs, dangerously close to becoming the victim of its own success. At a time when there is the greatest clamor among students for admission to the university there is the greatest dissatisfaction with the conditions of student life and studies. ... At a time when research is richly supported – and respected – it is being described as the academic Trojan Horse whose personnel have all but captured the city of intellect. And at a time when faculty members are in greatest demand for service around the world, there are intimations that their efforts to save the world will cost us our university soul.[16]

The paradoxes described by the former president of Cornell University have become even more acute in the quarter century since this observation was made. The success of the modern university in technical research and professional training has been more than offset by its failure to provide a liberal education which guarantees only the opening of minds, not of jobs. A higher education that can be the basis only of spiritual riches, not of material profits cannot find favor in the context of a materialistic ethos. The current restraints in government funding for many non-utilitarian programs like philosophy, classics, fine arts, music, and the reallocation of resources to specialized technical training and research is, therefore, an inadvertent assault on intellectual literacy and higher education.

It would seem that a higher proportion of public sector funding needs to be directed towards promoting liberal education programs in colleges and universities in order to correct the imbalance that has been created by several years of neglect. Higher education can then come into its own by aiming at intellectual literacy rather than limiting itself more and more to specialized academic literacy and professional training – which are mistakenly called higher education. Private sector funding, with reasonable tax incentives, would then have to assume even greater responsibility than it now does for promoting research and development based on specialized academic literacy, as well as for professional and technical training programs needed to fill the jobs in the industry. Such a division of labor in funding would assure the necessary promotion of both mind-power and manpower – of education and innovation.

Yet, we must not make the mistake of confusing the necessity for such basic support and funding for liberal education programs with the current notion that the quality of higher education is necessarily an increasing function of the tax dollars poured into the educational system. In fact, it is another paradox of the modern university that increased funding has actually had the adverse effect of scuttling liberal studies in favor of more and more specialized, professional, technical and vocational programs. As one time U.S. Secretary of Education, William J. Bennett, noted in his address on the occasion of the 350th Anniversary of his alma mater, Harvard University: "Money has meant growth and expansion, which in some places has meant a diffusion and loss of focus, a loss of central purpose."[17] Thus, in becoming a victim of higher funding, higher education has lost its central purpose and focus on liberal studies, and has instead promoted the growth and expansion of utilitarian post-secondary education.

Universities across the continent now perceive themselves to be in a state of crisis because of the present cutbacks in public funding which endanger the growth and maintenance of high-cost academic programs. While such a crisis may represent a danger for the expansionist tendencies of post-secondary education, it does represent a definite opportunity for the comeback of higher education which fosters intellectual literacy. Academic institutions that are still capable of rethinking their educational aims and reinstating liberal studies, which form the heart and soul of higher education, may actually become educationally enriched by such relative institutional poverty!

This double-edged nature of academic funding, with its potential for cutting positively for post-secondary education and negatively for higher education, becomes a dilemma only on the assumption that all academic institutions must try to model themselves as multiversities whose success is measured by the range of their offerings. Finding such a trend appalling even in its relatively early stages during the mid-fifties, Robert M. Hutchins was extremely blunt in his criticism:

> The infinite proliferation of courses is repulsive. There is a good deal of evidence, ... that the education system as a whole needs *less money* rather than more. The reduction of its income would force it to reconsider its expenditures. The expectation that steadily increasing funds will be forthcoming justifies the maintenance of activities that ought to be abandoned; it justifies waste.
>
> Some waste is inevitable; but the amount that we find in some universities is disgraceful. These institutions carry on extravagant enterprises that by no stretch of the imagination can be called educational, and then plead poverty as the reason for their financial

campaigns. The self-interest of professors, the vanity of administrators, trustees, and alumni, and the desire to attract public attention are more or less involved in these extravagances. Yet the result of them is that the institution is unintelligible, and, in every sense of the word, insupportable. [Emphasis added.][18]

— VI —

Excellence in higher education need not be expensive if the academic institutions can exercise realistic restraints in their expansive tendencies. Professional and technical training, on the other hand, can be an expensive affair depending on the means employed in such training. The tools of training are often the latest high-tech gadgets with both a high price-tag and a high rate of obsolescence, while the tools of education are long-life and low-cost books, although "a good book", as the poet Milton put it, "is the precious life-blood of a master spirit." The transfusion of thought and wisdom that takes place through reading the great books of such master spirits has become even more important in our technical world which confuses education with training, the useful with the valuable, and the latest with the best.

However, any proposal for reforming education using the 'great books program' needs certain qualifications that have been best articulated by Mortimer Adler, who has championed the cause of liberal education for more than half a century. Adler rightly notes that such a program is not satisfied by a few courses in the history of Western civilization, nor is it meant to be a scholarly study of great books. The primary concern of such a program is the discussion of great ideas and issues explored in these books – which means that it involves a "dialectical teaching of students" rather than a "doctrinal teaching of disciples." Adler sums it up with his characteristic clarity:

> A genuine great books program does not aim at historical knowledge of cultural antiquities or at achieving a thin veneer of cultural literacy. On the contrary, it aims only at the general enlightenment of its participants, an essential ingredient in their liberal education and something to be continued through a lifetime of learning. ...

The educational purpose of the great books program is not to study Western civilization. Its aim is not to acquire knowledge of historical facts. It is rather to understand the great ideas. ...

We read them for the light they throw on the fundamental ideas that no century has outlived and the perennial issues that no century can avoid.[19]

What we call the great books are those works of philosophy, science, literature and art which deal in intellectually challenging ways with the universal ideas of humanity and reflect the perennial problems of human existence. The greatest of these works are those that have raised the most profound questions and explored the deepest meanings of human experience relating to the place and role of humanity in the cultural-cosmic fabric of existence. It is the combination of the universality and inexhaustibility of such works that constitutes the ultimate touchstone of their greatness. While universality has to do with a book's cross-cultural recognition, inexhaustibility has to do with the influence that a book exercises on those who follow. For instance, the philosopher Whitehead was using such a criterion in the case of Plato's works when he observed that "all philosophy has been a series of footnotes to Plato." Similarly, the richness and complexity of the philosophical system of Immanuel Kant had provided so much grist for the mill to so many shades of philosophies and philosophers who followed him that it inspired poet Schiller's ode to the "joy" of Kant: "See how a rich man has given a living to a number of beggars."[20]

Moreover, the timelessness of the ideas and meanings in the classical works are in direct proportion to the inexhaustible hold they have on our minds, which does not end when we finish reading them. Their reach therefore must exceed our grasp, or what are great books for? We may say with Aldous Huxley that such books are indeed "the proper study of [hu]mankind." Yet, we may now have gone far beyond Mark Twain's well-known quip that a classic is "a book that people praise, but don't read" – since many modern universities seem to have even stopped praising them.

Education is a process of continuous awakening that comes from the pursuit of the intellectual virtues of knowledge, understanding and wisdom. Ideally, education must foster humanization – the art of living humanely and wisely, and the judgment for appreciating truth, beauty and goodness. Such education is best obtained from the critical examination and discussion of basic ideas and issues found in the great works of humanity – ancient and modern. In fact, antiquity and modernity no longer seem to be valid distinctions as we become familiar with the knowledge, understanding and wisdom displayed in the works of the ancient philosophers, poets and playwrights.[21] It almost seems, as Mark Twain once put it, that "the ancients stole all our ideas from us!" Amazement is followed by humility when we learn that the ancients are really very modern, and that antiquity is really a prejudice of the moderns, not simply a bygone chronological event which can be counted out for all present and practical purposes. None of this applies to training, which involves the mastering of the latest research techniques, and the learning of currently useful technical skills that provide gainful employment in a trade or a profession.

Higher education, centering on liberal studies, does not have the utilitarian value of training since it deals with knowledge and understanding for their own sake. Such a vision of liberal learning forms Michael Oakeshott's idea of a university:

> This, then, to the undergraduate, is the distinctive mark of a university; it is the place where [students have] the opportunity of education in conversation with [their] teachers, [their] fellows and [themselves], and where [they are] not encouraged to confuse education with training for a profession, with learning the tricks of the trade, with preparation for future particular service in society or with the acquisition of a kind of moral and intellectual outfit to see [them] through life. Whenever an ulterior purpose of this sort makes its appearance, education (which is concerned with persons, not functions) steals out of the back door with noiseless steps. The pursuit of learning for the power it may bring has its roots in a covetous egoism which is not less egoistic or less covetous when it appears as a so-called 'social purpose', and with this a university has nothing to do.[22]

Liberal learning is thus a participation in what is called "the great conversation" of humanity which has been going on ever since the ancients became aware of the power of ideas in the pursuit of knowledge, understanding and wisdom. The great books are those in which the greatest minds of humanity have carried on this rich tradition of intellectual conversation down the ages. Their works thus embody profound and enduring ideas of humanity that are easily submerged in the mass of information to which we are exposed every day of our lives. Academic amnesia even prevents the resurgence of such ideas in those fragmented mini-conversations of the specialized researchers – euphemistically called "learned conferences." Liberal education is a means of providing a retreat from the commonplace in order to allow entry into the company of the great thinkers and artists who hold up to us what the philosopher Alfred North Whitehead called "the habitual vision of greatness." It is by conversing with and about their works, and by participating in their vision and wisdom, that we can re-evaluate our thinking and thus elevate our own minds to loftier planes.

The timeless truths and universal values, which are embodied in the classics of human intellect, not only elevate our minds but also serve as mirrors in which we may confront the many sides of our own humanity. There is yet another reason why such an approach is critical for us. A liberal education can be truly liberating only to the extent that it can break the stronghold of the present on our minds. Courtesy of modern technology and the media, the demands made on our attention by our increasingly complex and informationally overloaded environment have stretched and widened what Augustine had called "the present time of things present." When the present becomes so powerful, the past is inevitably lost to our consciousness. Such shrinking of consciousness to a single dimension thus spells the gradual extinction of historical consciousness – allowing sensationalism and barbarism to become the order of the day. "Released from all authoritative past", says Philip Rieff, "we progress towards barbarism, not away from it" for "barbarians are people without historical memory."[23]

Such barbarism appears to be one of the chief characteristics of most academic institutions which have strayed away from the ideals of a wholesome education that nourishes the soul. Thus more and more institutions today provide the kind of education which impoverishes the soul by catering merely to a runaway technology and to the bread and circuses in demand for the day. The decline and fall of higher education, and intellectual literacy with it, is inevitable where there is historical amnesia. Paul Woodring's warning is thus most appropriate in this context: "All the dark ages that blot the pages of the history of our own and other civilizations began when the older generations failed – for one reason or another – to transmit the cultural heritage to the young."[24]

With its present-centered focus on specialisms and utilitarian programs, post-secondary education actually facilitates historical amnesia. Higher education based on liberal studies counters such historical amnesia by focusing on the appreciation of the intellectual and literary wealth generated over the long course of human history, and by promoting the critical examination and understanding of the great ideas and the significant works of humanity, which continue to have a bearing on the problems facing us in the present. Besides providing a comprehensive understanding of our intellectual heritage, such an education serves both to enhance the shared experience of the educated, and to combat the knowledge fragmentation that runs rampant in our institutions of higher education today.

Of course, the present trend is in a direction that is unquestionably harmful to the kind of higher education which would provide a humanizing and liberating experience. The sort of leisure that is filled with busywork is not conducive to a continuous conversation either with our peers or with the peerless masters of the past. On the academic assembly-line such conversation purely for the non-utilitarian purpose of edification can be hazardous to one's professional health, since it constitutes potential interference with what is called 'productivity'.

Historical amnesia for the intellectual tradition, combined with the productive-cum-futuristic orientation of a technological society, makes it almost impossible for politicians, parents, progressive presidents and professors to pay more than lip-service to any kind of education that is not utilitarian through and through. The incontrovertible fact is that the economy itself is now being driven mainly by technological knowledge and innovation, which have had a significant impact on the manufacturing industries of yesteryears. Such an economy reinforces the sort of education which provides specialized technical training to run the technological engine that powers the economy.

The technological requirements of the modern industry are based on a combination of specialization and organization which facilitate both the predictable planning of the technostructure and its resulting achievements. In a competitive technological society, marketability guides training, research and development, so that it is not at all surprising that both the public and private sectors would favor specialized training over a well-rounded education. In becoming victims of the technological ethos, most modern academic institutions have thus reneged on their mission to provide a higher education that is geared to the elevation of the mind.

Perhaps all this is simply nostalgia for an academic golden age. Indeed, as Richard Stivers has observed, "The high culture of the past [itself] survives as nostalgia, rather than as a living culture that informs everyday existence." Mass media in general, and television programs and advertising in particular, have literally manufactured the popular culture which, according to Stivers, "is the only national culture, especially in light of the fact that the ruling class is more a technical class than a cultural class." Moreover, he adds, "infatuated with the new and the sensational the media unintentionally destroy the sense of the past."[25] However, since "shared experiences and a sense of the past are a motivation to conserve what is best," it is not difficult to attribute to the media a major share in destroying the best that has been thought and said in the past. Consequently, universal liberal education in such a popular culture may be no more than wishful thinking.

Perhaps we should no longer be too reticent about declaring the intellectually superior nature of liberal education. Such a conception would not be inconsistent with democratic or egalitarian ideals of the freedom and dignity of each human being, since these qualities are concerned with social, political, legal and moral equality, not intellectual homogeneity. By implication then, if not by definition, higher education cannot be mass education. That the capacities and qualities of mind involved in such intellectual education are distributed evenly among all the citizens in a democratic society is highly improbable, if not impossible.

In fact, given our pluralistic society, a utilitarian ethos and a complex technological environment, it may no longer be wise even to entertain the possibility of making intellectual literacy a prime requirement for all college and university graduates. Given the prevalence of academic specialization, it may even be impossible. Substituting a smorgasboard of specialized courses in different disciplines offered by specialist professors is not a recipe that can foster intellectual literacy. Liberal education is an approach to the world of knowledge, the goal of which is best characterized by the Greek word *paideia*, or by the Latin expression *humanitas*. These terms refer to the kind of broad and general learning which enables an educated individual to make critical judgments in most branches of learning, not simply in one specialized branch of a single discipline. Mortimer Adler gives a succinct definition of the product of liberal learning: "The mark or measure of a generally educated human being is that the individual should feel comfortably at home in the whole realm of learning."[26] Or, at least in a realm large enough to include philosophy, science, history, religion, literature, and fine arts.

We have strayed so far away from such an ideal that there is a fairly low probability of finding such generally educated individuals in our academic institutions today. A high degree of intelligence, talent and training we do indeed find, but not education measured in terms of general intellectual literacy. This rather embarrassing paradox of modern academic education seems to rest on the discomforting possibility that students are almost certainly acquiring an inclination for intellectual illiteracy from specialist professors. Both pupil and professor know that, in our present technological society, specialization spells success, whereas a generally educated human being frequently has to take a vow of relative poverty.

It seems to be another paradox of our times that, despite the increasing dependence on narrowly trained experts, the spell of specialisms has weakened to some extent in the wake of the electronic media which keep the masses up to date with comprehensible lay-packages of specialized information. Thus, while busy experts continue with time-consuming research to gain more specialized knowledge, in many instances, the average person today may be more widely informed – courtesy of the television and all the media which have become the medium of our very existence.

Such access to wide bodies of information has indeed created a generalized public awareness of the advances made in several different departments of knowledge. However, it is not clear how such "awareness" translates into real understanding for those who do not have the kind of higher education which enables one to make at least some critical judgments in evaluating the significance of the information presented by experts.

The rate of turnover in the informational commodities churned out by the knowledge industry is so high that integrated thought has been largely displaced by fragmented information. Ironically, the extensive dissemination of vast amounts of uncoordinated information seems to turn into noise almost as inexorably as the law of entropy itself. Jeremy Rifkin makes an ominous observation on the perils of information overload:

Strangely enough, it seems that the more information that is available to us, the less well-informed we become; decisions become harder to make, and our world appears more confusing than ever. ... As more and more information is beamed at us, less and less of it can be absorbed, retained and exploited. The rest accumulates as dissipated energy or waste. The buildup of this dissipated energy is really just social pollution, and it takes its toll in the increase in mental disorders of all kinds, just as physical waste eats away at our physical well-being.[27]

Information overload is equally harmful for intellectual literacy, which focuses on the total context of the whole realm of human knowledge and experience for purposes of fostering integrated thought rather than a fragmented mind. Not surprisingly, therefore, John Ralston Saul's list of 'Voltaire's Bastards' includes the specialized professors who "devote themselves to the prevention of integrated thought" by turning the universities into "temples of expertise."[28] Thus, when judged on a scale of integrated thought, rather than one of specialized knowledge or informational turnover, modern academic education fails to qualify as higher education.

ᐁ— VIII —ᐅ

As if it was not already enough of a problem dealing with matters like reducing information overload and despecializing the academic towers of babel, universities for some time have been in the vanguard of a cultural coup d'état on intellectual literacy which has led to a virtual bedlam in the groves of academe. The very idea of a university and the ideal of higher education seem to be in the process of being almost completely deconstructed by the absolutist demands of a variety of relativistic and nihilistic interest groups – which, in vying for a place on the academic curriculum, seek also to displace with a vengeance the whole tradition of liberal studies on the alleged grounds that it is steeped in racism, patriarchy and ethnocentricity.

Besieged by the politics of race, gender and culture, the universities have become political hotbeds for ideologues – some of whom are ready to scrap the very intellectual foundations of higher education in the interest of equal representation and intellectual egalitarianism. That liberal education in the West does indeed have an over representation of the ideas and works of white, male Europeans cannot be denied. But neither is there any need, nor any point, in apologizing for the course that human history has taken down the ages. If great and gifted minds have made permanent and monumental contributions to human thought by bequeathing their valuable insights and experiences to the annals of human knowledge, art and literature, it makes little difference whether they were male or female, white or black, European or Asian. Indeed, white male Europeans happen to have contributed a profound and significant amount in many departments of human knowledge and imagination, but it would be ludicrous to hold this against them, or against those who would want higher education to expose them to the best that has been thought and said in the world. In fact, such recognition represents a truly liberal tradition of universalism, not parochialism, or white patriarchal Eurocentrism – as the deconstructors of liberal education would have us believe.

Ironically, it is pure parochialism to believe that we can only understand other cultures, races or nations through Asian Studies, African Studies or Canadian Studies, and the female gender only through Women's Studies – programmed by the ethnic and gender experts. In fact, apart from the patronizing tone in many of these claims, such compartmentalization and differentiation of experience and knowledge into area studies is also a species of inhumane specialization which divides rather than unites. Such divisiveness, especially at the undergraduate level, can only promote what has been called "illiberal education" – which imprisons the mind within the rhetoric of ideologies, instead of freeing it with liberating ideas.

The danger in the "cult of ethnicity" running amok, as Arthur Schlesinger Jr. has rightly observed, is that it "exaggerates differences, intensifies resentments and antagonisms, [and] drives ever deeper the awful wedges between races and nationalities. The end-game is self-pity and self-ghettoization." However, Schlesinger does not rule out teaching about non-European cultures: "Let us by all means teach Black history, African history, women's history, Hispanic History. But let us teach them as history, not as filiopietistic commemoration. The purpose of history is to promote not group self-esteem, but understanding of the world and the past, [and] respect for divergent cultures and traditions... ."[29]

Moreover, such ethnic navel-gazing may indeed be self-defeating, as Harold Innis had speculated: "Perhaps the obsession of each culture with its uniqueness is the ultimate basis of its decline."[30] A broad-based liberal education, on the other hand, frees a person from what Robert Hutchins called the "prison-house" of "class, race, time, place, background, family, and nation" – and 'gender,' he would indeed have agreed were he writing today in the midst of the sex wars.

The current academic thrust towards ethnic, gender and race-related area studies reflects a zeal for correcting all existing political, social, economic and educational injustices perceived to be distorting our civilization. Many academic revolutionaries even allege that liberal education based on the recognized masterpieces in the Western tradition is the prime culprit in promoting ethnocentric pride, patriarchy and racism – when such liberal education has never even been tried on a broad enough scale. In fact, it is the paradox of such area studies that they entail moving away from the traditional curriculum of liberal studies that can actually play a critical role, not only in correcting injustices and in advancing civilization, but even in promoting the meeting of the West and the East. In fact, there is neither East nor West when the intellectually educated stand face to face. On this matter, the eminent Eastern scholar, Ananda K. Coomaraswamy, has perhaps made an extremely wise comment:

> If ever the gulf between East and West, of which we are made continually aware as physical intimacies are forced upon us, is to be bridged, it will be only by agreement on principles. ... A philosophy identical with Plato's is still a living force in the East. ... Understanding requires a recognition of common values. For as long as men cannot think with other peoples, they have not understood but only known them; and in this situation it is largely an ignorance of their own intellectual heritage that stands in the way of understanding and makes an unfamiliar way of thinking to seem "queer."[31]

It is the recognition of common values, rather than differences, that leads to genuine understanding. Differences need to be protected and respected, but they can neither serve as a basis nor as a bridge for the shared understanding of our common humanity – which makes us all brothers and sisters under the different shades of skin color. However, appreciation of one's own tradition provides both a sense of tradition and a vantage point for the appreciation of other traditions.

In following up on Coomaraswamy's line of thought, Hutchins notes the irony in the demand for such area studies:

> The irony here is that those who talk most about the need to change the course of study in order to promote understanding of the East would be those who would proclaim most loudly the obsolescence of those parts of the Western tradition ... which are perhaps equivalent, with some transformation, to the important parts of Eastern traditions. Such people would vigorously oppose an education requiring everybody to try to understand those things in the West which have the best chance of leading to a genuine understanding of the East; but for all that they vigorously propose that we understand the East.[32]

Global understanding has become critical as well as timely in a world which is shrinking on a daily basis with the constant expansion of communication and transportation technologies. Yet the plea for the relevance of education to its times must be weighed carefully. Another perceptive scholar, Louis W. Norris, was concerned about the "grave danger" of such a plea – lest the timeliness of education were to obscure its timelessness:

> But the very reason they [Socrates, Plato and Aristotle] were able to make such helpful comments about social, ethical and political questions was, that they were even more concerned to find out the 'forms' of things that were timeless. Without the 'definitions' of Socrates, the 'ideas' of Plato and the 'forms' of Aristotle, their 'radio commentating' would have been shallow gibberish, forgotten as soon as ninety-nine per cent of present commentary. A frantic concern to understand Russia or the Orient will lead us nowhere, unless the student brings to these problems skill in analysis, order in valuing, knowledge of history, and such social experience as gives him a basis for judging what he finds out about Russia and the Orient.[33]

All this clearly points to the fact that liberal education is even more imperative in a world endangered by racism and ethnocentrism. In fact, paradoxical as it may seem, it may be the only antidote to the divisiveness that continues to be promoted by the ideologues of special area studies based on race, ethnicity, gender and nationality.

In a tribute to his "Beloved Author, Mr. William Shakespeare" the playwright Ben Jonson said: "He was not of an age but for all time." It is this universal attitude that we gain from any rational assessment and imaginative understanding of the great works – which are not only for all time but for all people all over the world, too. Thus our intellect and imagination are raised to new levels of awareness whether we read the great dramatic works of Aeschylus, Sophocles, and Euripedes (who championed the cause of women's emancipation in ancient Greece), or those of Molière, Goethe, and Ibsen (who also championed women's liberation); whether we study the ideas of Socrates (who had high respect for Aspasia, the live-in companion of Pericles), Plato (who kept positions open for women in the highest ranks of his ideal society, which was based on meritocracy rather than on employment equity), and Aristotle (who was the only male chauvinist among the big three), or those of Nietzsche, James, and Freud (whose work championed the emotional and sexual liberation of both men and women); whether we read the essays of Montaigne, Bacon and Emerson, or the poetry of Milton, Blake and Whitman; whether we read the satires of Cervantes and Swift, or the psychological insights of Balzac and Dostoevsky. All these works of white male Europeans, and many more, are not of an age but for all time – like Aesop's Fables which contain universal wisdom, as Socrates, Plato and Aristotle all seem to have known so well. The fact that there are translations of all these masterpieces in almost all the major languages of the world is in itself evidence that they must deal with universal themes and values which transcend both historical and cultural differences.

Likewise, for Michelangelo, great works of art always participated in the world of ideas by representing the eternal behind the temporal. As two historians of art, Bruce Cole and Adelheid Gealt, also observed, "art can embody and transcend both its creators and its times to reveal enduring truths about the human condition" so that "the more we understand art, the more we understand ourselves and the complexities of our world." "For its particularly human orientation," they add, "the art of the West has an important place in the history of civilization" and is "one of humankind's most glorious achievements" for "in it flows the spiritual and intellectual lifeblood which still nourishes and sustains our ancient civilization."[34] Thus, despite the artistic treasures of the East, there are no artists in any age or culture who are comparable to such creative geniuses as Leonardo, Michelangelo, Titian, Raphael, Rubens, or Rembrandt. A similar claim may be made about the music of the West. Despite the musical richness of the East, there are no composers in human history who are even remotely comparable to Bach, Haydn, Mozart or Beethoven.

However, the far and near East have had more than a fair share of incomparable artists of life – Moses, Jesus, Mohammed, Buddha, Confucius, Lao Tzu, Zoroaster – immortal spiritual teachers who have animated the history of humankind with universal and timeless truths. There is also the incomparable poetry of the Persian trio Omar Khayyam, Saadi and Hafiz (the last two of whom had a powerful impact on Emerson), the transcendental poetry of Jalaluddin Rumi (whose 'Mathnawi' was much admired by Goethe and Hegel), the poetry of Rabindranath Tagore (whose 'Gitanjali' so deeply moved W.B. Yeats), and the writings of the middle Eastern poet-philosopher Khalil Gibran – whose works continue to enjoy a wide audience in the West. Not to be overlooked is one of the most celebrated story books of all times known as *The Thousand and One Nights* or the *Arabian Nights Entertainment* with tales which seem to have a striking similarity to some Biblical tales and to the events in the *Iliad* and the *Odyssey*. Introduced to the West in the eighteenth century, these tales not only captivated the popular imagination, but also inspired the exquisite music of Rimsky-Korsakov's *Scheherazade* as well as Lord Alfred Tennyson's *Recollections of the Arabian Nights*.

The East has indeed made a profound contribution to the enrichment of intellectual thought, religion, art, literature and culture. It is thus not surprising that at least some of this was also known to many of the eminent thinkers in the Western tradition – from Pythagoras and Plato down to Schopenhauer and Nietzsche. It is also not surprising that Will Durant's multivolume story of civilization begins with the volume on *Our Oriental Heritage*, while Aldous Huxley's *Perennial Philosophy* begins with Hindu philosophy. Claims of any sharp dividing line between Western and Eastern civilizations have turned out to be less than half-truths, based either on parochialism or historical amnesia. The intermingling of culture and thought is not a side effect of modern melting-pot or multicultural policies, but a fairly ancient phenomenon – as a scholar of Eastern languages and civilization, Thomas Cleary observes:

Grecian culture and thought are universally acknowledged to be among the main roots of Western civilization, and the inspiration of the European Renaissance. Grecian cultures and philosophies were originally of considerable variety and were also commingled with other cultures and ways of thought, including the already ancient as well as the contemporarily current. Elements of Minoan, Egyptian, Chaldean, Indian, Persian, and Hebrew cultures were absorbed by inquisitive Greek peoples over the centuries, producing dynamic new syntheses.[35]

Western civilization is thus not as purely Western as it has been made out to be except in the fictional accounts of cultural separatists.

Interestingly, the modern West has learned much about Oriental works from the writings – commentaries and translations – of many recent Western scholars who were clearly steeped in the tradition of liberal education. The works of Western scholars, from Max Muller to Heinrich Zimmer, have done so much to initiate interest in the Eastern contributions to religion, philosophy, science and art that one may confidently state that possibly most students and scholars in the West and the East today better understand and appreciate the East due to their familiarity with the writings of the Western scholars who have studied the East, notwithstanding their so-called "orientalism" – which culture critic Edward Said believed to be rooted in a romanticized, yet condescending and intellectually imperialistic attitude towards the Orient. However, it is by their intellectual fruits that such works should be judged now, not by their attitudinal roots.

In the face of such incontrovertible evidence, the so-called cultural conceit and provincialism of the West is no more than a myth – as Barzun emphatically observes:

> It is the West, and not the East, that has penetrated into all parts of the globe. It is only the West that has studied, translated, and disseminated the thoughts, the histories, and the works of art of other civilizations, living and dead. By now, the formerly shut-in peoples do take an interest in others, but this recent development is in imitation of Western models. By good and bad means, Western ideas have imprinted themselves on the rest of the world, and one result is that cultural exchange and mutual interaction are at last consciously international; this, just at the time when we are told to repudiate our achievements and consign our best thoughts to oblivion.[36]

That the multicultural assault on the intellectual-literary heritage of the West is entirely without any foundation has also been observed by Roger Kimball in his study of the politicization and corruption of higher education by the tenured radicals:

> There is something grimly ironic about the spectacle of our new multiculturalists using ethnocentricism as a stick with which to beat the West. After all, both the idea and critique of ethnocentrism are quintessentially Western. There has never in history been a society more open to other cultures than our own; nor has any tradition been more committed to self-criticism than the Western tradition: the figure of Socrates endlessly inviting self-scrutiny and rational explanation is a definitive image of the Western spirit.[37]

In fact, the interpretations and commentaries of many Western scholars remain decisive in unraveling the essentials of important non-Western works which are embedded in a different cultural context. Needless to add that such understanding of the East can only enrich liberal education programs and promote 'the meeting of East and West' – to use the expression of the Western scholar F.S.C. Northrop. However, the crucial point here should be obvious. It is the tradition of liberal education in the West which has been responsible for the genuine openness to the non-Western contributions, and has led to such excellent scholarship about the East. The conflict between an exclusive emphasis on the Western tradition in liberal education and a flight into a cafeteria-style multicultural curriculum, with emphasis on current ethnic literature, can be resolved through a reconstruction of liberal education simply by incorporating some of the significant works and contributions of the East into its curriculum. Humane learning can only be based on the understanding and appreciation of the full range of the human tradition. Nothing human should be foreign to us, à la the Roman playwright, Terence; so that we should consider the whole world to be our culture, as the great Flemish artist Peter Paul Rubens believed.

Intolerance, prejudice and discrimination are a function of closed minds. Liberal education is the best remedy for opening such minds because its approach and content transcend the boundaries of age, race, culture, gender and nationality. For instance, is there the slightest possibility that someone would even think for a moment about eliminating the *Confessions* of St. Augustine from a liberal studies program if they perchance learned that he had some African blood in him? Has the origin of the Bible itself in the culture of the Near East made any difference to its profound impact on Western consciousness? Have Western scholars refused to study Buddhism because its founder belonged to an ancient culture and happened to have Indian nationality? Did the ancient Greeks need a policy of affirmative action before attributing wisdom to the female goddess Athena? Or a building policy on gender equity to dedicate to her a temple that was one of the finest examples of Doric architecture?

Even a cursory examination of works included in a good liberal studies program shows up the fictitious nature of the criticism claiming that such a curriculum is inherently gender-biased. For instance, there are those who would see Shakespeare's play *The Taming of the Shrew* as inherently misogynistic. Thus, even while observing that some of Shakespeare's heroines like Portia were "learned women, reflecting the somewhat higher status of women in that period," Riane Eisler goes on to add that "the treatment of Shakespeare's heretically rebellious Kate in *The Taming of the Shrew* and other literary works indicates [that] the violent reassertion of male control was already underway"[38] even before the Elizabethan age was over. Such critics overlook the possible subtlety with which the master playwright may have been showing how the battle of the sexes can result in a win-win situation of equality – especially when 'taming' involves, as G. Lloyd Evans observed, "a recognition that the reality of love is more important than outward word and show" and that within the total truth of love, "such things as honor, obey, and submit, are not bits and snaffles, but wings." 'To love, honor and obey' thus turns out to be an excellent recipe for equality, not subordination. The apparent misogyny in the play is thus redeemed by what Evans calls "a celebration of the mystery of love's wealth."[39] There are far richer and deeper meanings in the plays of Shakespeare than are dreamt of in ideologies that look only at the surface.

Moreover, while Shakespeare's exact identity has been a matter of some debate over the years, no one has yet suggested that he may have been a woman. However, even knowledgeable feminists would not deny that he showed an unsurpassed understanding and appreciation of both the male and female souls – and even a genuine admiration for the more integrative attributes of the feminine in his later plays – as one well-known feminist scholar, Marilyn French, has recognized. French concluded her illuminating examination of Shakespeare's division of experience in words that express the universality of the Bard of Avon:

The work of Shakespeare has been a major influence on all of Western culture. The world does not need me to say how much we owe him. He expressed, often in great poetry, the feel, the texture of human life on earth, the explorations and conclusions of a large, generous, and probing mind. He never settled for the received idea even in the area (sex) where it had most deeply implanted itself. He never turned his back on power, that uncomfortable subject. And he never stopped searching for a way to reintegrate human experience.[40]

In more recent times, the feminist vilification of Freud and psychoanalysis is likewise a result of ignorance and irresponsible scholarship. On the other hand, in what is perhaps the most knowledgeable critique, the feminist scholar Juliet Mitchell writes:

> The greater part of the feminist movement has identified Freud as the enemy, ...Psychoanalysis is seen as a justification for the status quo, bourgeois and patriarchal.... but the argument of this book is that a rejection of psychoanalysis and Freud's works is fatal for feminism. However it may have been used, psychoanalysis is not a recommendation *for* a patriarchal society, but an analysis *of* one. If we are interested in understanding and challenging the oppression of women, we cannot afford to neglect it.[41]

If we set aside irresponsible Freud bashing, there can be no doubt that the social and political liberation of women in our own time has been profoundly reinforced by Freud's work towards the emotional liberation of women. In fact, in its unique blend of clinical discoveries with the insights of poets and philosophers, Freud's depth psychology remains one of the most searching examinations of the human psyche ever undertaken in the course of intellectual history, and one of the most profound commentaries on the all-too-human in the annals of knowledge. As Norman Brown observed: "To experience Freud is to partake a second time of the forbidden fruit."[42] Freud's contribution to our understanding of human nature is thus far too significant to be ignored in any liberal education program.

Nor may we neglect the fact that many of the foremost male European thinkers and writers have also fully appreciated the feminine principle in life. For instance, towards the end of his life, the consummate German philosopher-poet, Goethe, finally concluded the second part of his classic work, *Faust*, with words that show a mystical appreciation of the feminine: "The Eternal-Feminine draws us onward" – perhaps toward the same infinite perfection of love which, in Dante's concluding lines of the *Paradiso*, "moves the sun and the other stars." While at least some great male poets seem to have recognized their Jungian anima, many critical feminists continue to struggle with their animus – even as male European supporters of the Western canon, like Harold Bloom, dare to question the Mosaic authorship of the oldest strands of the Bible, the so-called bastion of patriarchy, and propose the possibility of an erudite female author.[43] However, gender itself is not a decisive criterion for any creative work, as Georgia O'Keefe observed: "There is no man's art or woman's art, there is just Art."[44]

Based on such exemplary evidence, one can indeed say that only they serve humanity best who, by going beyond the limits of gender, race and culture, develop their intellectual and spiritual powers to their highest capacity and bestow upon the whole of humanity the gift of their truly universal knowledge, understanding and wisdom. Paradoxically, therefore, it is in the very context of a white patriarchal society that some of the greatest male minds of humanity have shown an intuitive knowledge and appreciation of the female psyche and feminine values, even as they exposed the many vices of the male psyche – such as power, greed, lust, envy and ambition. A Eurocentric liberal studies curriculum therefore goes beyond the limits of gender, race and culture as it embraces the diverse deeds of the human spirit and the myriad meanings of human experience. To dismiss such a curriculum with sham charges of ethnocentrism would be to ignore the most profound works of those very writers and thinkers who probed and unravelled the secrets of the soul and the mysteries of the mind. Only such a liberal studies program can rise above the socio-cultural prejudices of the day. No one but a woman of such extensive scholarship and breadth of mind as Camille Paglia could have so brilliantly exposed the underlying hypocrisies of the feminist critique with such astounding brevity:

> The very language and logic modern woman uses to assail patriarchal culture were the invention of men. ... One of feminism's irritating reflexes is its fashionable disdain for "patriarchal society," to which nothing good is ever attributed. But it is patriarchal society that has freed me as a woman. ... Let us stop being small-minded about men and freely acknowledge what treasures their obsessiveness has poured into culture.[45]

Of course, this includes the treasures of the East like the *Upanishads*, *Bhagvad Gita*, *Tao Te Ching*, *Confucian Aphorisms*, and the *Rubaiyat of Omar Khayyam* – to name only a few. Yet, despite all such incontrovertible argument and evidence, uncivilized debate on these issues continues unabated in the halls of academe, where a literate culture of intellect and imagination is fast being replaced by a literal culture of relativistic and nihilistic deconstructionism – a culture which provides a collectivist stronghold for the nurturing of illiberal education and intellectual illiteracy. In such a totalitarian culture, it is not surprising that academic freedom has given way to academic license and academic anarchy – which threaten both intellect and imagination.

Almost as if he were writing today about the inquisitorial censorship of the politically correct illiberal education, the former President of Yale University, Alfred W. Griswold, wrote what is perhaps the most succinct defense of liberal education:

> Books won't stay banned. They won't burn. Ideas won't go to jail, ... In the long run of history, the censor and the inquisitor have always lost. The only sure weapon against bad ideas is better ideas. The source of better ideas is wisdom. The surest path to wisdom is liberal education.[46]

Liberal education is also the surest path to intellectual literacy. Conversely, all forms of illiberal education constitute an inadvertent assault on intellect.

Chapter 3

• •

The Academic Assault on Intellect

*Why has the American college and university so little connection
with Intellect?*

> - Jacques Barzun
> *Foreword, The Academic Marketplace*[1]

With the devaluation of intellectual literacy and its confinement
to the wings on the stage of higher education, it is not at all
surprising to find so little connection between university and intellect.
This lack of connection seems to reflect the anti-intellectualism that
some acute observers have found to be so prevalent in much of North
American society. Such a supposition, however, assumes that a
university is simply the society writ small – which in some ways it is;
it also implies that what is not honored in a society will not be fostered
in a university – which also makes a great deal of sense. Of course, the
causal influence may also be viewed as running the other way, so that
a prima facie case may be made for suggesting that a society is its
educational system writ large. This is indeed a plausible assumption
considering the fact that, at least in modern Western societies, most of
the leaders in government, business and industry whose thinking exerts
a pervasive influence on society are often the products of post-secondary
educational institutions – which would tend to imply that what is not
fostered in the university will not be prevalent in society.

Thus the university and society have indeed been locked over the
years in a mutual process of making each other into mirror images –
which may also help to explain the growing similarity that we witness
between academic institutions and other social institutions like
government, business and industry. For instance, increasing

bureaucratization, power politics, committees, conferences, collectivist thinking, assembly-line training, the mass production of research, reports and administrative memos are a few examples of a shared modus operandi. It is no secret that academics were among the willing victims of this process of transformation of the university from its traditional role as a beacon illuminating our intellectual heritage to a role in which it simply mirrors societal trends. With such a conversion in roles, the intellectual and critical functions of the university could not but wane over the years.

In losing the critical function, the university has become just another institution where career advancement, conformity and busy-work assume priority over intellectual literacy. Critical thinking and writing which enrich the knowledge and imagination of a whole culture could not thrive in a culture of academic experts and technicians whose esoteric discourse was incapable of providing any such intellectual edification. Thus Irving Howe rightly observed that, in losing their traditional critical role, academics "cease to function as intellectuals" and therefore it is no longer possible to "accept the notion that the academy is the natural home of intellect." In the same vein, historian H. Stuart Hughes noted: "We are living in a society and in an era where there is scope for comparatively few intellectuals."[2] Hutchins had passed the same judgment as Howe and Hughes two decades earlier when he observed that "the modern temper produces the strangest of modern phenomena, an anti-intellectual university."[3]

After being brewed for years in the same melting pot as the rest of society, it is not at all surprising that the North American university has remained in a state of near perpetual identity crisis – buttressed by conflicting views of higher education. A unified vision of the university as a "temple of intellect" seems to have all but disappeared. Thus it is not so much the "worship of intellect" that is of concern to us now, as it was to Henry James Sr. in the nineteenth century, but the decline of intellect in the university and in society.

Intellectuals had come to the university for several good reasons besides May, June, July, August, and the seventh year sabbatical bonus. Intellectual life supposedly suffused all the classrooms and corridors of academe. Post World War II years gradually exposed the myth of the university as the hub of intellectual activity. The growing social recognition and utilization of academic research was indeed a cause for elation among many of the otherwise reclusive inhabitants of the ivory tower. With research and development taking a firm foothold in the universities, empiricism and specialisms overwhelmed intellectual life.

These and other developments became a cause for serious concern among leading intellectuals like Philip Rieff, who observed:

> Attracted to the university by the new money and status in it since 1946, the bagmen and gurus between them are destroying our sacred institution. Both sides are equally ready to make the temple of intellect into whatever it cannot be: research and development, political camp, college for therapists.[4]

Of course, over the years, research and development have become the pride and joy of most universities – almost the equivalent of the Holy Writ. Many universities also serve as havens for activism, although the terms of the debate have shifted from 'relevance in education' and 'student power' to 'political correctness' and censorship of critical thought – with an intense focus on issues relating to racial, ethnic and gender victimism.

Such an ideological climate could not but promote a militancy that far surpasses all earlier forms of academic power politics. The whole Western intellectual tradition, and all remnants of the liberal arts programs which support this tradition, are thus dismissed as outmoded forms of racist, sexist or ethnocentric ideology. Not surprisingly, the most conspicuous feature of this new debate is that it does not purport to be a debate at all, as it often sidesteps intellectual analysis or rational criticism – which are perhaps considered to be merely Eurocentric modes of thought. Thus the specter of the thought police is not only hostile to the freedom of thought and speech, but it is literally an attempt to drive intellect itself out from its own temple by collectivist forms of harassment and intimidation on the part of the more radical and vocal ideologues.

～ II ～

The trend towards the democratization of higher education, as manifested in mass education, especially since World War II, has hastened the devaluation of liberal education and the erosion of intellectual literacy. With the continuing politicization of higher education, combined with the empiricism and specialisms promoted by academic research and development, the anti-intellectual bias prevalent in the larger society has been further entrenched within the walls of academe. General liberal education is certainly not consistent with specialisms. Nor is intellectual literacy compatible with studies that reflect a curriculum guided by resolutely non-rational forces demanding equal representation for accidentals like color of skin, culture and gender. Only when the academic curriculum is intellectually weighted, and guided by ideas based on the constants of human nature, can it prevent intellectual life from simply withering away in the competition of interests inherent in such egalitarian pluralism.

Alvin Kernan describes the crisis of confidence in literature in his provocative exploration of the collapse of American literary and artistic culture:

> The great historical tradition extending from Homer to the present has been broken up in various ways. What were once masterpieces of literature, the plays of Shakespeare or the novels of Flaubert, are now void of meaning, filled with an infinity of meanings, their language indeterminate, contradictory, without foundation .... Rather than being near-sacred myths of human experience of the world and the self, the most prized possessions of culture, universal statements about an unchanging and essential human nature, literature is increasingly treated as authoritarian and destructive of human freedom, the ideology of the patriarchy devised to instrument male, white hegemony over the female and the "lesser breeds."[5]

All such trends have had a perilous effect on the curriculum of higher education. Intellect is not compatible with either ideology or bureaucracy – both of which suffocate thought. Nor need higher education be an organized democracy of pluralistic interests, with continuing political activism on university campuses. As Sidney Hook explains:

> The fact that a society is politically organized as a democracy does not entail that all its other institutions be so organized – its families, its orchestras, museums, theatres, churches, and professional guilds. I think that we may expect all the institutions in a political democracy function in a democratic spirit, and by that I mean that all the participants of any institution should be regarded as persons, should be heard, listened to, consulted with. But ... the responsibility for decision cannot be shared equally without equating inexperience with

experience, ingnorance with expertise, childishness with maturity. The assumption of political democracy is that each citizen's vote is as good as any other's. If we make the same assumption about universities, and define a citizen as anyone who functions in any capacity on the campus, we may as well close up educational shop.

[Moreover] ... no full-time activist can acquire a liberal-arts education of a depth and breadth commensurate with his talents, for the simple reason that there are not enough hours left in the day for study and reflection after the caucuses, meetings, demonstrations, and news conferences are over.[6]

While this may seem more applicable to the student activism of the sixties, it actually describes a general malady which seems to run rampant in most North American academic institutions. Almost all administrators, many faculty members, and more than a few students seem to have a potent propensity for democratically organized committees. "Outside of traffic", Will Rogers had said "there is nothing that has held this country back so much as committees." Undeniably, universities have also been held back by the senseless proliferation of committees vulnerable to political and ideological manipulation by academic careerists with non-intellectual aims. Given the fixed number of hours in a day, study, reflection and teaching cannot but suffer. Of course, for the want of critical reflection, intellect itself is lost.

Moreover, intellect cannot be democratized without a loss of its critical edge. In a political democracy, one person implies one vote, equal in value to all other votes. However, in the temple of intellect, each individual does not imply an intellect of equal value to all other intellects. It is precisely in recognition of this fact that we place the works of outstanding intellects at the core of a liberal studies program. In fact, individual variations in breadth and depth of intellect place it beyond the egalitarian philosophy and totalitarian politics which dominate the academic marketplace today. A.M. Sullivan expressed the elitist conception of intellect very succinctly: "After all, it is a poor democracy that cannot afford a little aristocracy, especially the aristocracy of a searching and generous intellect."[7] Likewise, Rieff expresses the elitist conception of a university in no uncertain terms: "A university is neither a political democracy, nor an oligarchy; it is an intellectual aristocracy."[8]

ᴄᔆ— III —ᔆᴄ

Increasingly, then, the connection between intellect and university has been strained over the years to the point where it seems necessary to reflect briefly on the nature of intellect and the conditions under which intellectual life is fostered within and outside the halls of academe. Accordingly, it is necessary at this stage to qualify the meaning of intellect in contrast to other related capacities of the human mind.

Intellect may be defined as the critical and reflective power of knowing that operates conceptually and connectedly in the realm of ideas and meanings. Thus it can only be shaped by the proper kind of education. On the other hand, *intelligence* may be defined as the general mental capacity to learn that is essentially adaptive and utilitarian. Thus training and experience determine its direction and application in a variety of situations. Unlike intelligence, which is trained for useful, adaptive and problem solving purposes, intellect is cultivated by the kind of education that may often seem superfluous. For instance, the ideas of philosophy have no survival value, but they give shape and substance to intellect.

Using intellect simply as a generic term for mental operations such as understanding, judging and reasoning does not convey its full import, since such operations are also involved in many evidently non-intellectual activities and situations – from home-building to hotel-management training. Equating intellect with intelligence, or with a problem-solving ability, is problematic from the point of view of usage. For good reason, we do not speak of a highly intelligent child as a great intellect. Intelligence is best estimated quantitatively on a high-low scale, while intellect can only be judged qualitatively in terms of its metaphorical 'breadth' and 'depth' which are acquired only through a proper form of education. Thus, genius may be one percent inspiration and ninety nine percent perspiration, as Thomas Edison once put it – but in his own case it may have also been almost one hundred percent pure intelligence. There seems to be more than a grain of truth in that old adage that intelligence is what enables one to get along well in life without an education. Likewise, equating intellect with trained intelligence is also problematic – for it then confers the status of 'intellectual' on every technician whose intelligence has undergone highly specialized training in any human endeavor, as well as on every highly gifted chess player. Yet, a master mechanic or a grandmaster would not be regarded as a great intellect simply by virtue of having such talent or trained intelligence.

In this sense, we may distinguish the famous inventive and commercial geniuses like Edison, who thought religion was all bunk, and Ford, who thought history was bunk, from such highly educated creative geniuses like Freud and Einstein, who were also great intellects – deeply versed in history, philosophy, religion and literature. Whereas the ideas of Edison and Ford changed the way we live in the physical world, Freud and Einstein changed our ideas, and thereby the way we think about ourselves and the world. Thus, in the realm of intelligence, ideas serve as useful tools in adaptation or invention, whereas in the realm of intellect ideas are the very objects of thought and understanding – although many ideas such as liberty, equality and fraternity may also exert a powerful influence in the conduct of our lives. Accordingly, Einstein's equation $[E = mc^2]$ is a feat of intellect, while the making of the atom bomb was a technical application of intelligence, like Edison's light bulb and Ford's model-T.

In fact, at an intuitive level, we do seem to recognize the essential distinction between intellect and intelligence when we speak of artificial intelligence or thinking machines. It is the utilitarian problem-solving nature of intelligence, and even the logical thinking attributed to reason, which can be artificially mimicked at a high level of efficiency in computers programmed by human intelligence. While, in this sense, intelligence and logical thinking can be artificially imitated, intellect cannot even be vaguely simulated in a non-human contraption. To speak of artificial intellect, then, would be as absurd as to speak of an artificial human being, since intellect is the power of knowing which operates in the context of a human tradition of ideas, meanings and metaphors. This is the reason why those whom we call great intellects are original and reflective minds of powerful imagination who have contributed profound ideas, meanings and metaphors to our human tradition. Obviously, then, whereas intellect itself is inconceivable outside the intellectual tradition of humanity, intelligence is present in varying degrees even in non-human forms of life.

Thus intellect is embedded in an intellectual tradition where the very ideas defining human existence are themselves the objects of thought and study. Since intellect is both integrative and reflective, it can be properly cultivated only by the kind of higher education which is based on a critical examination, understanding and appreciation of such general and vital ideas in the great intellectual works of humanity down the ages. Such ideas serve as the common currency of intellect in both its rational and imaginative modes – *reason* being the special ability for logical thinking necessary for making reliable and valid judgments, and *imagination* being the special ability for creative and visionary thinking which extends the horizon of human consciousness even as ideas deepen one's understanding.

In the rational mode of intellect, ideas serve to invest experiences and events with meaning and significance, and make possible logical analysis, integrated understanding, critical judgment and coherent articulation. In the imaginative mode, ideas act as aids in the formative powers of conception and creation, making possible the creative works of philosophy, science, art and literature – the greatest of which have eluded both scientific explanation and formal academic education or training. Nevertheless, it is the reflective study and appreciation of ideas in the great works of creative intellect that is the key to cultivating the imaginative mode of intellect – also called intellectual intuition.

Of course, ideas serving the rational mode of the intellect are also learned in a similar process of education, whether the educational setting be the Athenian agora or the modern academy, a public library or a personal one – as long as there is both opportunity and leisure for reading and reflection, as well as for periodic live dialogue. Since it is reflective thought based on reading that seems to promote intellect best, there can be no real foundation for cultivating the intellect in any true sense of the word without leisure both for reading the great works – which awaken thought and imagination, and for reflection – which promotes appreciation and understanding of the great ideas in the intellectual tradition.

It is thus worth reiterating that the hallmark of liberal education is a critical examination of the significant ideas and creative works of human intellect for the sole purpose of promoting reflective thought and cultured imagination. A liberal education program, which makes provision for such a comprehensive approach to the development of intellect, would therefore have to consist of a good combination of core courses in philosophy, science, history, religion, literature and the fine arts – and a study of some of the cardinal ideas and works in each of these disciplines. Such liberal studies, properly grounded in the history of ideas, provide an integral understanding and appreciation of the various aspects of the natural and human world. Only such an education can serve the function of truly liberating the mind both from ignorance, and from the forms of prejudice that have recently taken on racial, ethnic and gender overtones in our strife-torn universities.

While liberal education is a prime requisite for the cultivation of intellect, it is not a necessary condition either for enhancing the general capacity of intelligence or for reinforcing the rational and imaginative abilities – since reason and imagination are also employed in the varied operations of intelligence. Thus one can also become highly trained, well-informed, and technically skilled in any profession or trade without such liberal education. Yet, without a cultivated intellect and an educated imagination, which are conceivable only in the context of liberal education, much of academic knowledge and training remain considerably impoverished in their intellectual, moral and spiritual value.

This is true even in an age where educational success is measured in terms of professional, technical or vocational preparation. In such a practical and materialistic context, the testimony of one who rose to the pinnacle of financial success is most heartening. Writing about his own education, Jean Paul Getty writes:

> My exposure to a wide variety of liberal-arts subjects made my mind more flexible, more receptive to new ideas, more readily aware of changing circumstances and, at the same time, more convinced of what constitutes real and lasting values. I do not hesitate to state flatly that I consider my liberal-arts education to have had far greater overall importance than any of the purely technical or professional subjects I studied.[9]

As Getty also saw, there are only two choices in academic education: one can choose to be a "narrow specialist, little more than a technician, concentrating entirely on the useful disciplines and disdaining all else," or become a well-rounded person "of taste, discernment, understanding and intellectual versatility." Liberal education thus provides the critical concepts and categories for understanding and appreciating the world, thereby enhancing our experience of it. The paradox of modern academic education lies in the fact that its specialist-technical-professional-vocational bias has itself become the greatest obstacle to fostering a culture of intellect.

Without such a culture, the very possibility of intellectual life is jeopardized, as Louis Wirth had observed more than half a century ago:

Despite the fact that the Western world has been nourished by a tradition of hard-won intellectual freedom and integrity for over two thousand years, men are beginning to ask whether the struggle to achieve these was worth the cost if so many today accept complacently the threat to exterminate what rationality and objectivity have been won in human affairs. The widespread depreciation of the value of thought, on the one hand, and its repression, on the other, are ominous signs of the deepening twilight of modern culture.[10]

Albert Schweitzer had expressed a similar concern: "Today there is not only a neglect of thought but an actual distrust and depreciation of it."[11] The value of thought in our modern universities is depreciated both by the vocational training of one-dimensional professionals and technicians for a specialized job market in a technocratic society, and by the rhetoric and slogan-mongering in a culture of ideologues and bureaucrats. Higher education proper is meant primarily for promoting the value of thought, and for disseminating the intellectual values which foster the growth of culture.

∾— IV —∿

Freud seemed to have had in mind just such a culture of intellect when he wrote to Einstein in 1932 saying that "whatever fosters the growth of culture works at the same time against war." For, in discussing the question of a world view only a year later, he was very specific: "Our best hope for the future is that intellect … may in the process of time establish a dictatorship in the mental life of man."[12] Some years earlier, Freud had noted something peculiar about the weakness of the intellect in comparison to instinctual life: "The voice of the intellect is a soft one, but it does not rest until it has gained a hearing. Finally after a countless succession of rebuffs, it succeeds." However, he realized that the "primacy of intellect" lay in a distant future, albeit "not in an infinitely distant one."[13]

Even such long-range optimism regarding the future of intellect seems questionable in a conformist and collectivist society which is guided by a strange mixture of technocracy and ideology, rather than by the critical power of intellect. Mass education combined with a market orientation produces philistinism, rather than an educated imagination; while the cult of information and ultra empiricism breed esoteric specialisms and divisions that erode the unified structure of the traditional programs of liberal education. With the prime emphasis on training and skills, tailored to the requirements of professionalism and vocationalism, it would be a miracle indeed if thought and reflection did not often take an almost invisible back seat in our modern anti-intellectual university.

A technocratic milieu has an inherent tendency towards organization and specialization, which are not only antithetical to an intellectual state of mind but also to nurturing genius. However, technocracy seems to promote the common public perception that the modern scientific-industrial achievements are the work of great intellect and genius. On this subject John Kenneth Galbraith strikes a contrary note in his terse remarks:

> This is pure vanity; were it so, there would be few such achievements. The real accomplishment of modern science and technology consists in taking ordinary men, informing them narrowly and deeply and then, through appropriate organization, arranging to have their knowledge combined with that of other specialized but equally ordinary men. This dispenses with the need for genius. The resulting performance, though less inspiring, is far more predictable.[14]

Thus, a technocratic organization seems to do away with the need for the potential genius of the individual intellect in favor of the organized intelligence of specialized groups, narrowly trained to solve technical problems. Eager to be full participants in technological progress, academic institutions promote technical specialisms at the expense of general liberal education. The resulting myopia and tunnel-vision have now come to pose a potent threat to the very survival of intellect in academia.

For purely intellectual reasons, technocracy and specialization prove disastrous. For, as Lewis Mumford observes: "to know more and more about less and less is in the end simply to know less and less." The result is Ortega y Gasset's "learned ignoramus" who "gives the name of 'dilettantism' to any curiosity for the generalized scheme of knowledge." However, while intellect itself is inconceivable without such a foundation in a generalized scheme of knowledge, idiocy is not ruled out – as Bernard Shaw quipped: "no man can be a pure specialist without being in the strict sense of the word an idiot."[15] Scholarly obscurantism and posturing witnessed in learned society meetings and in the learned journals is perhaps the most blatant manifestation of such idiocy today

Shaw's witticism regarding such specialized idiocy finds a parallel in Carl Bernstein's trenchant comments on idiocy in the popular culture:

> We are in the process of creating, in sum, what deserves to be called the idiot culture. Not an idiot subculture, which every society has bubbling beneath the surface and which can provide harmless fun, but the culture itself.
>
> For the first time in history the weird and the stupid and the coarse are becoming our cultural norm, even our cultural ideal.[16]

Courtesy of popular journalism and popular television, Bernstein notes, the public is being "stuffed with garbage" – which is characterized by "lack of information, misinformation, disinformation and a contempt for truth." Combined with entertainment, not to mention the internet, all this has led to the creation of "a sleazoid infotainment culture" in which readers and viewers are being taught that the "trivial is significant."

Likewise, everytime the students in our specialized universities are taught that the trivial is significant, we too breed idiocy in our academic culture. While universities have never had a monopoly on breeding genius, they now seem to be losing even their ability to promote intellectual development through higher education. Intellectual stimulation can be provided only by a focus on ideas rather than on research and techniques. Since intellect is literally shaped by the quality of ideas, the works of the great thinkers and their modes of inquiry need to be a central part of higher education. Early specialization, with its prime emphasis on technical skills, narrows the focus of education, and fails to awaken the intellect. Thus, premature training of students in specialized research techniques retards the development of an intellectual orientation, unless they have first had an extensive exposure to a generalized scheme of knowledge rooted in the historical framework of ideas.

The widely prevalent emphasis on developing skills in research and problem solving is based on the dubious premise that it would later enable students to do independent research and to improve upon received bodies of knowledge. While problem solving should be an intrinsic part of education from kindergarten on, research as it is generally conceived is best postponed until one has acquired sufficient familiarity with the origin, nature and significance of received bodies of knowledge during the undergraduate years. In fact, there is no better way to foster independent thinking than by devising a broad-based curriculum which requires an understanding of the works of those great independent thinkers whose ideas constitute our intellectual heritage. Without such a foundation of ideas that have literally shaped the intellect and the modern mind, academic education leaves the intellect in a dormant state, incapable of being activated by any amount of highly specialized research.

Thus, without an undergraduate curriculum that is capable of providing such a generalized scheme of ideas and knowledge, within the context of which students can develop a sufficiently intense interest in pursuing a given discipline, the intellectual aspects of higher education remain neglected. Noting such a trend in his observations on the American University more than a quarter century ago, Edward A. Shils had rightly concluded that "The multiplication of research students is thus, in part at least, a consequence of the neglect of the intellectual side of undergraduate education and contributes to its further neglect."[17]

Such neglect has become even more pronounced in recent years with the huge increases in the research labor force employed in the so-called knowledge industry – as the information industry is euphemistically called. Students interested in pursuing a given subject in any depth at the graduate level are therefore pushed even further in the direction of hyper-specialized research – which leaves the doctorate in philosophy with no philosophy, and only a facade of intellectual life.

The cult of information makes empiricism inevitable and breeds a plethora of professional specialisms catering to a wide variety of non-intellectual tastes. Such narrow-minded professionalism has its dangers, as Alfred North Whitehead had noted back in the mid-twenties:

> The modern professionalism in knowledge works in the opposite direction so far as the intellectual sphere is concerned. ... It produces minds in a groove. Each profession makes progress, but it is progress in its own groove. ... The remainder of life is treated superficially with the imperfect categories of thought derived from one profession. ... The dangers arising from this aspect of professionalism are great, particularly in our democratic societies. The directive force of reason is weakened. ... In short, the specialized functions of the community are performed better and more progressively, but the generalized direction lacks vision.[18]

"Perfection of means and confusion of goals"[19] is how Einstein had summarized the plight of the modern professionals and specialists. Now it is the academic specialists on various decision-making bodies who have weakened the directive force of reason with their seriously limited tunnel-vision of the intellectual mission of the university. While Viktor Frankl's observation was directed at scientific specialists, it seems equally applicable to all academic specialists: "What we have to deplore therefore is not so much the fact that scientists are specializing, but rather the fact that specialists are generalizing."[20] Is it any wonder then that the generalized direction lacks vision in both society and university?

Specialisms and subspecialisms also create a problem with the labels which are used for academic degrees. In no discernible way does a Master's degree in any discipline today reflect a mastery of the whole discipline itself – let alone any comprehension of the general scheme of knowledge. Nor does a Doctor's degree have any relationship to the original meaning of the term '*docere*' (to teach), and still less to philosophy. In fact, the Ph.D. today neither represents authority in one's own discipline, nor does it mean a highly educated or learned individual. Rightly has the narrowly specialized Ph.D. been ridiculed as a Phony Doctor! Ortega's 'learned ignoramus' has thus been the fastest growing breed in an academic context which continues to promote what he called the 'barbarism of specialization'.

— V —

The blind worship of technology, such as exists in our modern times, results in the sacrifice of intellect at the altars of professionalism and vocationalism. Excessive emphasis on research, technique and technical skills, rather than on thought and reflection, is indeed an extremely serious obstacle to the development of intellect – which is inextricably linked to the acquisition of a set of ideas that make up the intellectual tradition, and to the critical examination of the place of these ideas in the broad scheme of knowledge. In a technological society, therefore, the educational ideal is the intelligent and skilled technician, not the intellectual and scholarly academic or layperson of yesteryears.

The educational model of a technological society is thus consistent with both mass education and philistinism, but it is at odds with the intellectual and cultural aims of higher education. The consequent erosion of the culture of intellect has thus degraded education so much that, even with all the technological sophistication, much of what goes on in many academic establishments is not even at the intellectual level of programs on the Public Broadcasting Service. On the other hand, liberal education empowers the mind through intellectual enhancement and cultural enrichment, and liberates it from all forms of ignorance and prejudice so prevalent in our society. Furthermore, a critical appreciation of the general scheme of knowledge embodied in a liberal education program also constitutes the perfect catalyst for the actualization of the intellectual potential.

In his critique of science and culture over a century ago, Nietzsche had also addressed the issue of the adverse effects of mass education and technical specialization, as well as of the "despiritualizing influence of our current science-industry." The vast range of sciences, he observed, "condemns every scholar" to specialized labor in a limited sector and is "a main reason why those with a fuller, richer, profounder disposition no longer find a congenial education and congenial educators." Overemphasis on technological training and specialization in our own time has further weakened the spirit of such congenial learners, and the blame for this, of course, must be laid at the portals of our universities and their misguided scholars and administrators. Nietzsche makes this point with his characteristic candor:

> There is nothing of which our culture suffers more than of the superabundance of pretentious jobbers and fragments of humanity; our universities are, against their will, the real hothouses for this kind of withering of the spirit.[21]

According to the standards of an age that takes to mass education as naturally as it takes to mass production, Nietzsche's views indeed seem elitist:

> All higher education belongs only to the exception: one must be privileged to have a right to so high a privilege. All great, all beautiful things can never become common property.[22]

Obviously, Nietzsche's comments cannot be taken to mean that higher education is to be reserved for the economically or politically privileged, although this is precisely the direction in which we are presently going with the exorbitant increases in tuition costs for post-secondary education. If the educational task is to promote intellectual growth, it is necessary to provide exposure to the great works of human intellect and imagination. Since intellectual predisposition and interests are critical for this purpose, such an education would necessarily tend to be selective, not expensive. Ironically, the 'privileged' in this sense would be those who are resigned to the fact that a higher education cannot guarantee job openings, only the opening of minds, since it aims only at intellectual enrichment, not affluence or power – as it did in yesteryears. Thus, intellectual "elitism"/excellence is the necessary result of higher education; intellectual egalitarianism is a contradiction in terms, and contrary to fact.

Higher education can therefore be a meaningful enterprise only if it is based on intellectual aptitude and ability. As Rieff put it succinctly: "The only elite worth educating is one constantly open to the promise of intellect."[23] Jacques Barzun elaborates this point even further – albeit using a more general notion of intellectual aptitude:

> Rightly understood, there is nothing unpalatable about the facts of intellectual aptitude and nothing undemocratic or iniquitous about selecting the best for the highest training. Every citizen of this country understands the true principle perfectly well when it applies to Big League Baseball, the Army, science, or business organization. ...
>
> The truth is that the existence of superior brains does not touch in the slightest the theoretical bases of democratic government. Democracy in education is something very precise to uphold and work for. It does not mean "Everybody in college" or "One man – one A.B." It means, every man or woman freely endowed with a right to college education if he or she is previously endowed with the ability to profit from it.[24]

Of course, such a selective approach is already in operation in the high-demand colleges and universities. However, given the frequently ambiguous use of terms like "superior brains" and "selection of the best" for university education, it is even more necessary to maintain the distinction between 'post-secondary' and 'higher' education. It is common knowledge that most people with sufficient intelligence and ability [i.e. "superior brains"], but with little aptitude for liberal studies [interest in study of the great ideas], can and do profit greatly from post-secondary training aimed at preparing them for the work-place and expanding their job opportunities – which, of course, contributes to the raising of both personal and national standards of living.

Thus, other things being equal, the best are likely to do better in terms of success in life. However, if all colleges and universities become as pretentious in practice as they are in lip-service to selecting only the best and the brightest, some institutions will soon have to close shop. Given the fact that intelligence follows a more or less normal distribution in the population, it is inevitable that some colleges and universities will have to settle for working with varying numbers of more or less average students. Most academic institutions will do so out of sheer expediency, since it is far more convenient for presidents and professors to swallow their pretensions than to stand in unemployment lines along with those rejected students. Moreover, mass education, post-secondary style, is imperative now even for the average student merely to sustain the complexities of our economy and technology.

The need for selection on the basis of intellectual aptitude and interests really becomes critical only in the case of higher education based on a liberal studies program – which can only serve to enhance the quality of one's life and of the culture at large. In practice, however, selection has become a more serious issue in the case of post-secondary training, for which both cost and demand keep rising in tandem; whereas, in the case of higher education proper, attracting students rather than selecting them constitutes the major problem. This decline of interest in pursuing the path of higher education, which is committed primarily to the cultivation of intellect and to cultural enrichment, clearly seems to reflect a widespread obsession with the gross national product at the expense of the net intellectual refinement of culture.

High quality post-secondary training may produce an efficient technological society, but without the kind of higher education which molds the intellect, even the best of training by itself can only contribute to the further vulgarization of culture. Rieff's concern therefore seems well-justified: "The American universities are now producing tens and thousands of failed intellectuals and artists of life; this mass production may lead to the destruction of culture in any received sense."[25] Jacques Barzun puts it in an even more matter of fact way: "The worst danger is the creation of a large, powerful, and complacent class of college-trained uneducated men at the very heart of our industrial and political system."[26] It may already be too late as we sadly watch our university trained specialists and students preferring Dynasty over Dostoevsky, baseball over Balzac, hockey over Huxley, information over ideas, and surfing on internet over cultivating intellect.

⌒— VI —⌒

Mass culture is inhospitable to the aristocracy of intellect, just as mass education is incapable of fostering intellect. A combination of mass culture and mass education in our universities has thus produced academic philistinism – competence without culture. Disorder has been compounded even further by the pluralism of academic specialties and the relativism of ideologies in the social order. This mixture of specialisms and relativism has created a disturbing incoherence in our cultural consciousness, and a fragmentation of thought in the house of intellect – giving rise to much pseudo-intellectualism and post-modern unintelligibility, both within and outside the walls of academe.

Just as a culture of ideas seems to have been displaced by a culture of information and ideology, rationality itself has now been demoted to the status of just another perspective, merely one form of discourse, in our postmodern anti-intellectual universities. Thus it is a mark of sophistication in some scholarly circles to be able to deconstruct a text into as many subtexts as imagination permits – when it becomes dissociated from reason, and is completely unconcerned with sense and sensibility. Under such pretexts, leading oracles of postmodernism can get away with almost any perversions of thought – such as 'man' being an invention of recent date, just a "new wrinkle in our knowledge" about two centuries old, and about to disappear in the imminent postmodern era "as soon as knowledge has discovered a new form."[27] Thus, as one sympathetic critic has put it, "Man, as a universal category, containing within it a law of being, is, for Foucault, an invention of the Enlightenment … "[28] for purposes of establishing the political order on a rational and scientific understanding of human nature. Since Foucault believes such an enterprise to be hopelessly mistaken, he predicts the dissolution of Man in the near future. Of course, any such historical claim is fair game for one who rejects the idea of history as reasoned analysis based on notions of reality, identity and truth, but prefers instead to regard truth itself as merely what counts as true within a particular form of discourse. What we require in order to enter the post-modern era, Foucault believes, is to "renounce the will-to-knowledge" and "revere a certain practice of stupidity." Indeed! Many post-modern universities already seem to conform to such ideals. What we need to worry about, then, is not the 'end of man' but the demise of intellect and history, along with a rise in stupidity. For post-modernism seems to have deconstructed not only the intellect but history itself. It is, as Stanley Rosen put it, "the Enlightenment gone mad."[29] No wonder that Daniel Bell seems to have considered much of academic work to be the "leisure of the theory class."[30]

However, such postmodern sophistry regarding the relativity of truth has its historical precedence among the Sophists of ancient Greece – that is, if postmodernism allows us to assume the reality of such history. Relatively speaking, however, the ancient sophistic relativism was benign in its claim that "man was the measure of all things"; postmodernism, on the other hand, is nihilistic and makes 'man' a deconstructor of all reason.

It is also a well known truth of history that our modern Enlightenment interest in 'man' also has a precedent in ancient times when the wise Socrates tried to solve the new riddle of the Sphinx – What is man and his true function? – and located the law of man's 'being' in his psyche – i.e. regarding 'man' as subject, with his psyche as the seat of consciousness, and the source of intellectual-moral value and action. During this same period of intellectual awakening, we also find the Platonic attempt to establish a political order based on the understanding of human nature. 'Man' as a universal category is thus a discovery of Greek Enlightenment more than two millenia old, not a recent invention of our two hundred year old Enlightenment, nor a new wrinkle in our knowledge which is about to fade away into postmodern oblivion.

Camille Paglia's stinging comments provide one explanation for such apparent historical amnesia on Foucault's part:

> The truth is that Foucault knew very little about anything before the seventeenth century, and in the modern world, outside France. ... The elevation of Foucault to guru status by American and British academics is a tale that belongs to the history of cults. ...The more you know, the less you are impressed by Foucault.[31]

From the rise of modern philosophy in the seventeenth century rationalism of Descartes to the postmodern deconstructionism of Derrida, there is an obvious regression of thought and intellect from the rationally plausible "I think, therefore, I am" to an irrationally impossible "I deconstruct, therefore, I am not." When parodic imagination plays fast and loose with language to produce such schizoid distortions of discourse, intellect cannot but undergo a pathological deconstruction, which not only spells the end of humanist imagination, but also of the human mind as we have known it since the dawn of rational consciousness. 'Man' seems to have already disappeared in postmodern thought without knowledge having given us a new form. It would seem that it is such postmodern thought which is the new wrinkle needing to be ironed out of our discourse.

When discourse is divorced from the reality of meaning or object, and can mean anything or nothing, as in postmodern deconstructionism, intellect must necessarily become trapped in a surrealist prison-house of language. Like *a priori* relativism, deconstructionism is self-refuting when it is itself subjected to deconstruction. It may mean anything or nothing! Thus, deconstructionism itself turns out to be like a textual tale, told by a deconstructive idiot, full of sounds and signs signifying nothing. As such, it is destructive of reason and points the way to a tower of Babel.

In the process of pulling out both the rational and imaginative props of intellect, postmodernism has loosened the necessary bond between imagination and reason. As only an artist like Goya could have put it: "Imagination abandoned by reason produces impossible monsters; united with her, she is the mother of the arts and the source of their wonders."[32] When academic sophistry is guided by deconstructive unintelligibility, one can expect no more than those impossible monstrosities of thought which put reason itself to sleep.

Such abandonment of reason in postmodernism is also apparent in the "death of the author" as one leading postmodern "author" (?) called it.* However, there is a method in this madness according to two other leading postmodern "authors" whose authorial "existence" is equally questionable in view of their own position on the subject. One seems to believe that the authors are dispensable because what they write is not what they mean anyway, so that eventually it is the postmodern readers who literally write the text in the very process of reading it.** Never mind the unauthorized plagiarism! Another seems to believe that any kind of focus on the author is inherently objectionable since it not only places the reader at the mercy of the author, but also confers ownership and special status on the authors which implies power and author(ity) on their part.***[33] Honestly! What will they think of next?

Of course, it hardly seems to matter that by distributing authorship democratically, the voice of the now defunct author is muffled. In allowing for a multiplicity of subjective meanings, postmodernism literally makes the text itself into an ephemeral excuse for the meanderings of a postmodern reader's imagination, unbounded by reason. Much like Dadaism in art, deconstructionism stands for the celebration of irrational subjectivity and unlimited meaning. The truth of the ever present possibility of more than one interpretation in almost all exercises of intellect and imagination is thus trivialized into a blatant untruth claiming all fantasized and fantastic interpretations as equal truths, thus ruling out any possibility for the superiority of one interpretation over another. This is egalitarianism gone mad, since such radical relativism subverts the pursuit of both truth and meaning.

In fact, despite its modest egalitarian pretensions, relativism in any form turns out only to be a disguised form of absolutism, since the relativist has to assert the absolute truth of at least the principle of intellectual, moral or aesthetic relativism – on which no difference of opinion is permitted. Of course, if truth, goodness and beauty are merely in the eyes of the beholder, sanity in science and society become virtually impossible. That the alternative to relativism is not authoritarianism, but an appeal to the authority of intellect was therefore the focal point of the Socratic critique of the relativism of the Sophists (according to which each individual was the "measure of all things"). The subjectivist individualism of the post-modernist is based on an unscrupulous relativism, rather than on the rule of reason. This can only foster both unbridled irrationality and gratuitous irresponsibility, which can allow anyone to reject any inherent meaning, truth or value in any work of intellect and imagination, while permitting at the same time a rationalization of any outlandish fantasy as the interpretation of an emancipated post-modern imagination – emancipated, that is, from rhyme and reason.

The more specific dangers of postmodern relativism are unsparingly spelled out by Herbert London:

> Since relativism is in the ascendancy, students don't have to read primary sources. They are assigned Foucault's interpretation of the classics or Stanley Fish's analysis of the humanistic tradition. The disciplines have been eviscerated of rigor, and rely instead on the trendy. Structuralism, semiotics, Lacanism, and deconstruction are modes of thought pegged into intellectual fashion. They are devoid of real meaning, yet have the glow of superficial sophistication.

> Students repeat the psychobabble of instructors .... Derivative ideas drive the learning process in a mad quest for instant erudition. What one gets is the pseudo-sophistication of instructors leading the narrowly parochial and miseducated students.[34]

That such unintelligible discourse has become a mark of sophistication in some scholarly circles need come as no surprise, since much of academic work in the social sciences and humanities already borders on jargonized triviality and unintelligibility – albeit giving "the appearance of solidity to pure wind," as Orwell had said of political language.[35] The only redeeming value of all such discourse seems to be to keep the many politically and ideologically inclined academics gainfully employed. As one postmodern professor of humanities admitted, diverse avenues of research opened up by postmodern thought create "more work, in short, for academics" (!) by giving "more attention to the neglected and marginalized areas of our society" – such as the poor, the women, the gays, the black, the Hispanic and the Asian.[36] However, such diverse avenues of research have created a rather awkward situation in our postmodern university, where the dead authors of our intellectual tradition have now become the most neglected and marginalized of all people. If tradition is "democracy extended through time ... a democracy of the dead," as G.K. Chesterton put it, what could be more democratic than a liberal education that gives voice to the tradition of the dead? Unlike Huckleberry Finn, therefore, we do have to take "stock in dead people" – in this case as an investment in our own intellectual enrichment.

Had all this simply remained a game that academics played in their ivory towers, one would perhaps be amused, but not seriously concerned. In other words, it would be hilarious if it were not so serious. However, by insidiously filtering into much of academic and popular consciousness, postmodern thinking seems to have become a self-fulfilling prophecy threatening the end of rationality. One astute scholar of the subject, Pauline Marie Roseneau, defines the nature of post-modern consciousness:

> The post-modern individual calls for the end of certitude, reasoned argument, modern rationality, objective modern science, law grounded on jurisprudence, and art subject to evaluation on the basis of standard criteria. ...

If, as the skeptical post-modernists argue, there is no truth, no objective means to distinguish between right and wrong views, then only power remains for deciding whose perspective will prevail; indeed, women are among the groups that, historically, have had very little power.[37]

Without any possibility of a privileged perspective in post-modern thought, the underprivileged and victimized can only assert the superiority and validity of their creed by the politics of power – of which political correctness happens to be merely a tool of empowerment. However, the collectivist nature of such ideologies does not merely remain corrective, but quickly becomes both invasive and coercive. The academic consequence of such political correctness is a revisionist curriculum which irreversibly shifts the focus from liberal studies to issues relating to gender, race, oppression and victimism. One postmodern professor of humanities does not mince his words when he claims that "these changes aim to make politics a central category."[38] In the process, the postmodern university gets transformed into a political camp where the pursuit of truth is quickly displaced by the pursuit of power and piety – reflected in the proliferation of what has been called "illiberal education."[39] While mass culture has always been inhospitable to the aristocracy of intellect, post-modern thought seems to have completely subverted the culture of intellect whenever and wherever it has found a hospitable place in our institutions of higher education.

ᕱ— VII —ᕤ

Such an intellectual void in the postmodern university has made it more and more vulnerable to the forces of the market and the pressures of the state. Over the years, the demand for constant rationalization and modification of the curriculum has already led universities further and further away from liberal studies. Now, post-modern thought and anti-intellectual ideologies seem to have reinforced this erosion to a point of no return. At this stage, therefore, reforming education by tinkering with the curriculum seems no longer to be a viable alternative. Nothing short of a paradigm shift in the academic psyche is likely to take higher education back to its basics – rooted in the liberal studies.

However, the odds seem to be stacked against such a revolution in the academic and cultural psyche. For the New Age is not the Age of Intellect and Imagination which gave birth to science and technology; it is the Age of Feeling and Fantasy which science and technology have paradoxically made possible. Stivers finds an even deeper paradox: "Technology as the embodiment of instrumental rationality actually enlarges the domain and importance of the irrational (instinctual)."[40]

The more we require thinking to be done for us by intelligent machines and experts, the less the demand we need to make on our personal intellect for critical appraisal and judgment; the greater the technological affluence, the larger the scope for the free play of feelings; the more the products of technology cater to our fantasy, the less the need for engaging the imagination to project the possibilities of intellect.

In such an "amusement society," to use an expression of Saul Bellow, technological products themselves become part of an awesome cultural clutter which blunts the critical edge of intellect by debasing thought and language. For instance, the increase in television viewing, hand in hand with a decline in reading, has only led to our consciousness becoming fully saturated by desultory electronic images rather than being organized by a unified order of symbols. In the process, the very capacities of language, thought, reflection and imagination have all become appalling casualties. There seems to be evidence, Stivers points out, that "an increasing number of people, especially the heaviest television viewers, are losing their ability to think abstractly in and through language." Thus it is not surprising, as Ellul notes, that some people now think in largely emotional terms, thinking from image to image (or emotion to emotion) – which is found to be associated with a shrinking vocabulary.[41]

As Clarence Randall also noted: "Each advance in visual aids tends to soften our capacity to think for ourselves."[42] The ultimate advance in visual aids is now represented by virtual reality, custom made in cyber-space, and capable of satisfying the wishful projections of anyone simply by allowing the virtual deconstruction of reality itself. Thus, we may now be faced with the ultimate prospect of an irreversible softening of our capacity to think and to reflect on ideas.

This is also the Age of the Specialist-cum-Technician who, in turn, has produced the Information Age and the Cult of Information – both constituting obstacles to fostering the intellect, which needs a good primary grounding in the generalized scheme of knowledge provided by liberal studies. Reason and imagination can best be fostered through exposure to their highest forms of expressions in the works of human intellect. Thus, the current over-emphasis on the learning and application of research techniques in undergraduate education, combined with the obsession for training in the production and management of currently useful information, degrades the intellect by depriving the individual of the broad horizon of thought and imagination – and reduces the individual to "the level of a mechanic" as Einstein had warned.

'CompuThink' and 'InfoAge' are not only the dominant images in our technological society but also in most of our techno-political academic institutions. Almost insidiously, such a techno-culture alters the very habits of the mind, as Antonio de Nicolas explains so well:

> The culture of technology, shared by the faculty and imparted to the students, undercuts the mental operations of a free education for other shortcuts of the mind that avoid the accumulation of experience in exercising mental operations. Technological society believes in the instrumentation of reason – that is, it makes reason an instrument to achieve quantitative efficiency, in the name of which more rather than less is produced; universities become centers for the production, transmission, and storage of information... What begins as the intrumentation of reason, the narrowing and routinization of thinking, ends up as a habit by which all thinking is measured.... An education controlled by such habits of mind ends as the mechanization of education that allows no room either for freedom or dignity.[43]

Thus, even as we continue to pay lip-service to the traditional image of a university as a repository of our intellectual heritage of ideas, we are busy converting it into a computer depository for every trivial piece of current information. The sheer amount of such information can boggle the mind and paralyze the capacity to make rational judgments regarding the meaning and significance of the information. In fact, we go on confusing information with knowledge, even though the gap between them is obviously increasing at a phenomenal rate – with the most generous estimates being that increments in knowledge are approximately a cube root of increases in information. The immediacy of electronic gossip on the information superhighway of the internet can now further diminish the capacity for reflective and integrated thought. Intellectual decadence may thus be the ultimate price we will have to pay for such information overabundance.

Since specialization is both the cause and the consequence of information explosion, information and over-specialization together create the kind of academic atmosphere which has had an extremely injurious effect on the intellectual health of a university. However, what society and the economy do not value will not be promoted in a university. Thus, the so-called academic 'centers of excellence' are not havens of higher education, but useful Research & Development Academies in an unavoidable cause-cum-consequence relationship with the economy, industry and technology. However, when a university gets into such a lock-step with the economy, it cannot but march to the demands of the state and the market. The adoption of such a service-cum-servile role eventually erodes the critical edge of intellect, which is dulled by the massive tomes of specialized information produced under the banner of research and development.

Thus, however excellent and necessary such academic centers are for promoting growth and productivity through research and development, they cannot be brandished as models of higher education. It would be more in keeping with their mission to regard them as training institutes and think tanks for the industry, and/or academies dedicated solely to the technical application and advancement of disciplinary knowledge. This in itself is a full-time job today, given the complex bodies of information which are comprehensible to none but the specialized initiates – who, in turn, are incomprehensible to most outside their specialty, and irrelevant to students seeking the intellectual benefits of higher education.

Sadly, the fate of intellect in the halls of academe is now in a most precarious state as the educational competition between ideas on the one hand, and information and ideologies on the other, seems to be inclined in favor of the latter – given the sheer weight of information and the emotional appeal of ideologies. Critical reflection of ideas continues to decline as more and more technical resources are diverted to the efficient communication, storage and retrieval of information produced by specialized academic research, and more and more issue-oriented programs are introduced for the rhetorical inclucation of a variety of political agendas preached by the multiple "isms" now dominating many North American campuses. While information is filling up our minds, the ideologies are busy closing them. Universities are thus literally suffering from a syndrome which may be described as the closing of the over-filled North American mind!

Some of these trends were evident even four decades ago, as Harold Innis noted in his perceptive comments on the emphasis on factual information and the narrowing of professional education:

> Textbooks of systematized knowledge have been altogether too much in evidence. Courses have been carefully calculated with a view to the inclusion of all the relevant information during the three or four years of undergraduate work. The results have been a systematic closing of the students' minds. Initiative and independence have been weakened. Factual material, information, classification, reflect the narrowing tendencies of the mechanization of knowledge in the minds of staffs and students. Professions become narrow and sterile. ... Student and teacher are loaded down with information and prejudice. The capacity to break down prejudice and to maintain an open mind has been seriously weakened.[44]

The task of finding an opening for liberal education in such an academic atmosphere is further complicated by the bureaucratic mentality which has permeated so widely inside the halls of academe. Official planning and policies have come to occupy such a large share of academic time and energy that they leave little time for any kind of reflective thought. Bureaucratic language leads to bureaucratic thinking and a bureaucratic mind-set – which facilitates the use of slogans and routine solutions that enable the scholar to become entirely liberated from critical thinking. Intellect thus gets displaced by politics and rhetoric, while thought and judgment come to be dominated almost entirely by considerations of technique, quantification, efficiency, and visibility. Such routinization of thinking ends in the bureaucratization of education.

Bureaucratic institutions are inhospitable to intellect for a good reason. Intellect is essentially critical and, therefore, potentially subversive. Moreover, critical thought is incompatible with political correctness. Thus, neither the rituals of bureaucracy nor the dogmas of ideology can demand or obtain the allegiance of intellect. Conformity to either erodes the critical edge of intellect. Yet, frequent employment of this critical faculty of intellect in academia can be hazardous to one's professional career. Academics are thus caught between the proverbial devil and the deep blue sea, and seek solace in research and complacency – placing them beyond academic freedom and dignity. By repressing intellect, bureaucracy and ideology thus destroy the very integrity of a community of scholars who are reduced to the role of cogs in the vast bureaucratic-cum-ideological information industry – euphemistically called the university. Bureaucratic routinization of reason thus ends up with the mechanization of education – leading to the erosion of intellectual life in academia and to the promotion of an official climate of stupidity. "As far as bureaucracy is concerned," notes historian Paul Tabori, "the acquisition of authority more often than not leads to … an atrophying of the mind, to a chronic state of stupidity."[45] Not surprisingly, then, we often find a state of incurable trickle-down stupidity whenever authority rests in an academic bureaucracy. Bureaucratic over-management in a university thus endangers intellect in all conforming participants.

The common perception of university as a knowledge industry shows the power of both bureaucracy and technology in moulding our image of higher education. Such an image, however, has contributed immensely to the present academic malaise, although sociologist John Seeley noted the trend more than two decades ago:

> The basic business of the school from beginning to end is "the corruption of the young," in a sense opposite to that charged against Socrates. And the univesity crowns, perfects, and completes that process. …
>
> The university and the school system it crowns and culminates exist to civilize, and this is their moral mandate in the world, regardless of what "power groups" demand. This mandate or mission means precisely to take a given society, always fundamentally relatively barbarian, out into the light and onto the height. … The very peculiar but modern idea of knowing which justifies the reference to the university as a "knowledge factory" lies alike at the bottom of the sickness of a technology-ridden civilization, and of the troubles of the university conceived of as part of such a society. The protesting students very often know … that the "knowledge industry" is the primary locus for the destruction of men and the dehumanization of the social order. It is, as it stands, the velvet-gloved butcher of the spirit.[46]

The spirit dies, says historian Page Smith, "when the organizational structure of an institution of higher education is indistinguishable from a major corporation." Not surprisingly, therefore, "intellectual fragmentation and bureaucratic centralization" have become "the main themes of the university."[45] It is the abdication of intellect in such knowledge factories and educational corporations which unavoidably turns them into slaughterhouses of the human spirit. Unfortunately, however, most of the students today often do not realize the extent to which the whole system of university education dehumanizes them. They do not know because the anti-intellectual administrators and academics between them are too busy bureaucratizing education and scholarship with their lop-sided priorities – which supposedly serve the demands for government accountability, but primarily serve the dictates of the market, and of the many professional disciplines and the several pressure groups that have sprouted on campuses in recent years. Intellectual life itself has thus been frittered away in bureaucratic and pedantic details.

Higher education has been the inescapable victim of all such anti-intellectual developments. Like Humpty Dumpty, it has had such a big fall that not even all the academic men and women may ever be able to put the fragments back together again. Such fragmentation has proved to be no less than a deadly assault on the very integrity of intellect in the community of scholars – the inevitable aftermath of which could not have been anything other than the closing of the academic mind.

Chapter 4

• •

The Closing of the Academic Mind

Is an intellectual community possible in an age of specialization?
                                        - Robert M. Hutchins
                                          The Learning Society[1]

T he intellectual mission of the university can be fulfilled only if it remains a community of scholars with a shared basis of knowledge rooted in a historical tradition of ideas, which give shape and substance to the intellect. Incontestably, specialisms have eroded such shared knowledge by fragmenting the disciplines and disconnecting them from their historical context. Since tradition constitutes the very essence of a community, specialized academics uprooted from the intellectual tradition cannot be said to form an intellectual community at any given institution.

Giving primary allegiance to a discipline and receiving basic salary from an institution, the modern academic tries to combine the functions of teaching and research to satisfy both the institutional and disciplinary obligations. Any residual guilt for this partial commitment to the institution is made up partly by committee work and/or community service (which need even less thought than much of academic research), and partly by the arguable claim that teaching and research always go hand in hand, like love and marriage or horse and carriage – albeit such a claim becomes trivially true if one teaches only what one researches. However, given the extremely specialized nature of research, the highly touted 'marital' relationship between teaching and research becomes hazardous for undergraduate institutions professing to provide higher education based on liberal studies, which require a generalist-humanist approach to teaching.

In fact, given the competitive academic settings of today, research time does often expand, in keeping with Parkinson's law, to erode teaching time to a considerable extent – so that the research carriage leaves the teaching horse far behind! Such divided loyalties clearly seem to account for the generally observed phenomenon of a "flight from teaching." Moreover, allowing too close a connection between specialized research and teaching in higher education undoubtedly results in the kind of scenario that Bernard Shaw described with memorable brevity: "Though everybody seems to know the x,y,z of everything, nobody knows the a,b,c of anything."

Nevertheless, teaching, research, and service to institution and/or community remain the three obligations imposed on North American academics by contract and convention. Given individual differences in educational background and values, it is not surprising that academics have a variety of attitudes towards these functions. There are those who profess to love both teaching and research – but their solemn avowals often sound dubious. There are others who love teaching and hate research – but publish so as not to perish; still others who love research but hate teaching – even if they love the students. There is also a growing breed of academics who hate both teaching and research but love only committee work – especially the kind which makes penance possible by a profusion of public pleas for policies and philosophies ensuring commitment to teaching and research.

Of course, these categories do not exhaust all possible permutations and combinations. One category that cuts across all others is what one may call the institutional academic who is dedicated to campus politics, but damaging to intellectual life. Of course, politics becomes the mainstay for those to whom career advancement means climbing up the administrative ladder via busywork and committee work – until they reach their level of incompetence via the Peter Principle. Needless to add that such opportunistic academics, in collaboration with bureaucratic administrators, have contributed more than a fair share to the erosion of the intellectual community within the university. Guided solely by the politics of expediency, some of them have turned academic campuses into a strange mixture of a political camp-cum-corporation, where collectivist pressures take precedence over critical thought. When academic freedom and integrity are thus compromised, the intellectual community of scholars turns into a collective of careerists, researchers and ideologues.

There is also sufficient justification in attributing the demise of higher education to what Charles Sykes called "Profscam" – a scathing commentary in which Sykes charges the professors with polluting the intellectual heritage of society:

> Almost single-handedly, the professors – working steadily and systematically – have destroyed the university as a center of learning and have desolated higher education, which no longer is higher or much of education.
>
> … No understanding of the academic disease is possible without an understanding of Academic Man, this strange mutation of 20th century academia who has the pretensions of an ecclesiastic, the artfulness of a witch doctor, and the soul of a bureaucrat.
>
> His great triumph has been the creation of an academic culture that is one of society's most outrageous and elaborate frauds. It is replete with the pieties, arcane rituals, rites of passage, and dogmas of secular faith. …
>
> They have distorted university curriculums to accommodate their own narrow and selfish interests rather than the interests of the students. …
>
> They have cloaked their scholarship in stupefying, inscrutable jargon. This conceals the fact that much of what passes for research is trivial and inane.[2]

In academic life, too, truth often seems stranger than fiction. All the same, pursue it we must – whether it reveals itself or ourselves. Perhaps, as John Maynard Keynes noted in his succinct and pungent observation, education has become "the inculcation of the incomprehensible into the indifferent by the incompetent."[3] Undeniable as Profscam is, the academic reality is a bit too complex and variable to be painted so uniformly with the same brush. A critical understanding of this phenomenon requires some understanding of the variety of academic purposes and mind-sets that form the incoherently pluralistic knowledge industry.

Academic debates on most value-laden issues generally end up generating more heat than light – especially when the aims of higher education get obscured by the cliché which defines the purpose of a university to be the preservation, advancement and dissemination of knowledge. Of course, everyone takes all these aims for granted, and no one really seems to feel the need to examine these somewhat hackneyed terms defining the academic aims a bit more closely.

While the 'preservation' of knowledge has no ambiguity about it, even if it no longer remains the monopoly of the university, both 'advancement' and 'dissemination' of knowledge have dual meanings in the context of university education. Advancement could mean extending the knowledge of students through teaching, or advancing the body of information and knowledge through research. Similarly, dissemination of knowledge could mean disseminating advances in knowledge through teaching students, or disseminating new information or knowledge to other researchers through publication. In the case of higher education based on liberal studies at the undergraduate level, the first sense of each of these terms is clearly more meaningful, while at graduate level education, the second of each of these meanings makes more sense. Advancement and dissemination therefore have more to do with the teaching function at the undergraduate level, and much more to do with research and publication at the graduate level.

Only by recognizing such distinctions can we avoid turning undergraduate education into what it is fast becoming – a premature training academy in research techniques and specialized courses to prepare student fodder for faculty research and graduate school. While the growing number of specialized area studies – from Asian or Canadian Studies to Women's Studies – may be quite appropriate at the level of graduate education, they have become a perfect recipe for illiberal miseducation at the undergraduate level. Thus, just as students are beginning to expand their horizons beyond the television, they are introduced to the tunnel vision so widely prevalent among their mentors. To get back to Hutchins' question, then, it would be safe to say that an intellectual community of scholars is just not possible in an age of specialization. Hutchins himself did not mince words on this issue: "An intellectual community cannot be built out of people who are not pursuing intellectual interests."[4]

♋— II —♋

While the age of specialization was a necessary consequence of the expansion of knowledge, especially in the sciences, it had the paradoxical consequence of shrinking the horizons of both intellect and scholarship. As specialists and experts of all shades acquired academic power and prestige over the years, the university gradually ceased to be either an intellectual community or a community of scholars – although it continues to use these glorified descriptions, however outmoded they have now become. This is perhaps the only way to keep the specialists and students happy while they labor away under the illusion that they are still members of an elite community – albeit in a democratized institution.

However, there are at least two forms of academic "elitism" – the elitism of liberal education which does indeed promote an intellectually integrated community of scholars, and the elitism of specialist training which promotes its own diverse groups of academic experts. Haplessly, it was the elitism of tunnel-visioned experts which eventually gained acceptance and ascendance in most universities, allowing their empirical-quantitative methodologies and techniques in research and pedagogy to become the standard for judging scholarship and teaching – the aftermath of which has been the degradation of intellect in higher education.

Ironically, there was a method in this madness, and it was based on a whole program for the advancement of learning – proposed in the seventeenth century by Francis Bacon, but ignored by virtually all the great scientists from Galileo and Newton to Einstein in our own times. The empirical methodology on which so much specialist research is based, even in what currently pass as humanities, rests on the Baconian assumption that knowledge is simply the end result of process and method, not of intellect and imagination – nor any kind of individual or educational excellence. What could be more democratic than a method which, in Bacon's own words: "leaves little to the acuteness and strength of wits, but places all wits and understandings on a level ... and leaves little to individual excellence because it performs everything by the surest rules and demonstrations." A methodology which levelled all wits, and left so little to intellect and imagination also created a great deal of hack-work – "trifles achieved by great effort" as Bacon said in another context.[5]

It was precisely such hack-work that was largely responsible for multiplying the breed of researchers in our universities, and for promoting what Ortega had called the "barbarism of specialization." Thus a program based on an empirical methodology, proposed three centuries earlier managed to gain full ascendancy over all versions of liberal education based on a shared tradition of thought. Technique-generated information deposed intellect and imagination – which are fostered only by the ideational content of a liberal studies program.

In colleges and universities which profess to provide liberal education, academics need to spend time and energy on teaching and study in order to expand their mental horizons far beyond their own narrow areas of specialization. Such an ideal state of affairs certainly has an appeal for academics who are committed to the idea of a university as a place for the development of intellect by way of liberal education, especially at the undergraduate level. However, the process of corruption begins early in the lives of most academics in North American universities, where a misapplied publish-or-perish philosophy has remained alive and well ever since it was first inspired by the model of the German universities about a century ago. Woodring provides the proper historical rationale underlying the notion of academic productivity:

> The view that every professor ought to be a "productive scholar" was unknown to American colleges until they began emulating German universities in the late nineteenth century. The great German universities of that day (there were only a few of them) were graduate and professional schools with nothing comparable to our undergraduate colleges. Because there was often only one professorship in each department, the man who aspired to a chair could reasonably be expected to be a distinguished scholar who had made significant original contributions to his field.[6]

The blind and inappropriate imitation of this tradition in North American universities has led to a virtual tower of babel, with academics wasting a great deal of time on esoteric topics for the doctoral theses, and publishing papers on the basis of such research for securing a career. Thus unoriginal hack-work comes to be dignified as research, while insignificant research gets to be confused with scholarship. The academic temper of our times has ignorantly placed a perverse emphasis on the growth of a research-specialist mentality which subverts the cultivation of intellect.

Since research is tied to extrinsic goals such as tenure and promotion, the justification of research in terms of its necessity for teaching is often a convenient rationalization. Of course, such a claim is patently fraudulent in the case of undergraduate education based on liberal studies. While placing academics in graduate institutions under the burden of a publish-or-perish philosophy has led to an unwieldy overproduction of much trivial information, such a philosophy has proved downright hazardous in undergraduate institutions. Thus, many academics who continue to churn out research do so for survival purposes – reinforced by the bad habits acquired during their years of fairly specialized and discipline-oriented undergraduate education, followed by the blatantly over-specialized graduate school indoctrination.

Daring academics who attempt to escape the specialist trap by broadening their education and teaching perspective soon experience a rude awakening; they either face a bumpy career advancement, or the choice of another career. Universities with such lop-sided priorities and research-biased reward systems have actually discouraged the existence of broadly educated teachers with a good background in liberal education, while favoring the narrowly trained researchers in disciplinary specialities. Ironically, this is done under the preposterous assumption that such research makes for better teaching. As Woodring rightly observes, it is very doubtful that "the careful investigation of minutiae improves a teacher's competence to teach broadly liberal undergraduate courses as they should be taught." As he also notes, the sad fact is that the university is a poor place to look "if you want to find a man or woman who has read widely in many fields, and has had ample time to think about what he (or she) has read."[7] At best, the academic who is well and widely read is only honored as a dilettante.

On the other hand, what is generally ignored is the very obvious fact that, in the case of undergraduate liberal education, teaching in itself is a scholarly activity requiring reflection, interpretation, criticism and synthesis of large bodies of knowledge – all of which are hardly possible for those immersed in specialized research, committee work or campus politics. Such busy-bodies have to rely on second-hand textbook syntheses and publisher-supplied teaching manuals. In words that go straight to the heart of this matter, Paglia captures the professorial predicament, especially in the humanities, but equally shared by other disciplines:

> The number one problem today is not ignorant students but ignorant professors, who have substituted narrow "expertise" ... for breadth and depth of learning in the world history of art and thought. But there is no true expertise in the humanities without knowing *all* of the humanities. ... American professors have been institutionally impelled, by graduate education and then by the universities that employ them, to become

narrower and narrower. The goal of comprehensive cultural vision predicated by German philology, which esteemed universal scholarship, has been dismissed as unrealistic in a modern alienated world of fragmentation and subjectivity.[8]

Undergraduate liberal education, as Paglia rightly observes, requires "teachers and scholars who understand the history of civilization in broad, general terms." Barzun makes a similar point: "Teachers in college and university should be scholars. But scholarship and publication are not identical. Of the two, higher education should prefer scholarship."[9] That such teachers and scholars are conspicuous by their rarity in most of our colleges and universities is largely due to the fact that faculty recruitment has been based on expertise in specialized areas, while tenure and promotion policies have been based on publications – most of which involve quite trivial research in narrow segments of a discipline for the sole purpose of ensuring tenure and speeding up promotion. Thus, it is not difficult to see where we may place the greatest burden of responsibility for the erosion of general-liberal education in our universities.

◠— III —◠

While academics constitute a mixed bag of multiple roles in practice, closer observation reveals a few clearly definable types of academics. Even at the cost of simplifying a far more complex reality, it may still be worth identifying different academic orientations found among those whom we call researchers, scholars and intellectuals, and locating their mind-sets on a continuum from specialist to generalist. Despite occasional points of overlap at the working boundaries between them, we seem to be dealing here not simply with what would be different "representations of the intellectual" in Edward Said's terminology,[10] but with radically distinct orientations.

A brief comment may be necessary in order to clarify the somewhat unfamiliar use of familiar academic terms. Research and scholarship are often used synonymously, despite the fact that they usually have a specific reference to science and the humanities, respectively. However, neither synonymous usage, nor specific reference, seem to have legitimacy anymore. On the other hand, the general term 'intellectual' is used for all academics simply because they are all viewed as being equally involved in an intellectual enterprise. To suggest that such a belief may be no more than a myth is bound to invite the wrath of many academics. However, if the pursuit of truth is our academic mission, we cannot afford to be pusillanimous in our examination of even the most cherished academic image, namely, that all academics are intellectuals in the ideal sense of the word.

Regardless of the discipline, modern academic researchers subscribe to what we may call an information model, in which the prime emphasis is on the methodology and techniques for the collection, collation, and analysis of data. The sources of such information may range from the laboratory to the library. The very nature of such tedious work inevitably drives the researcher towards the kind of hyper-specialization that limits itself to a fairly narrow range of the discipline. Of course, this is quite understandable because, at the current rate of information explosion, no researcher can be expected to keep up with what's going on even in the rest of the discipline – let alone in other disciplines. The huge armies of highly trained and specialized researchers in the various academic disciplines may therefore be likened to the infantry – front-line foot soldiers performing fairly specialized tasks in their narrow trenches by using their technical competence to engage in the battle for information, usually without full command of a wider knowledge of even their own discipline.

Academic research thus provides us with information, of which only a relatively small proportion ever ends up having either general interest outside the university or any beneficial value to the public at large. Likewise, an undetermined portion of what goes on under the guise of basic research in the sciences may have minimal basic or applied relevance. Thus, if we are not to confuse between Ortega's "learned ignoramus" and the learned scholar, then we need to use the term scholarship to represent works of broader and deeper learning, rather than technical works in narrow segments of a discipline. Much of academic research, then, cannot be equated with scholarship for the same reason that we cannot equate information with knowledge.

Scholars may thus be defined by their wider disciplinary base, with interest in the analysis and interpretation of larger theoretical problems and conceptual issues for purposes of advancing knowledge in a broader sector of the discipline. However, depending on the subject under investigation, scholars may also engage in their own research, or use the information made available through research done by others. For instance, such scholarship-cum-research becomes necessary in the knowledge enterprise for purposes of testing important theories, new and old, or for organizing, analyzing and synthesizing facts in ways that throw some new light on theoretical problems and issues – usually of disciplinary significance and, therefore, of primary interest to other scholars. In fact, theoretical work even in the sciences may have now become an esoteric game, which one critic has called "ironic science" – free-style interpretations that are akin to post-modern literary criticism.[11]

While it may appear somewhat arbitrary to draw such distinctions between scholars and researchers, such an attempt nevertheless seems to be critical in appreciating the variety of mind-sets prevalent in academia. The least that such differentiation does is to prevent the inflated use of the term 'scholarly work' for every few pages of information generated by research – much of which makes it to one or another of the hundreds and thousands of so-called 'learned' journals floating around in academic circles, and collecting dust on library shelves. Research that becomes relegated to oblivion within short periods of time needs to be clearly distinguished from more enduring works of scholarship.

In the nature of the case, therefore, there is a far greater turnover of information than there is advancement in knowledge. The phenomenal rate of repeated displacement of old information by the new is reflected in the state of permanent boom in academic research publications – most of which become outdated even before publication. Since the reward system in most universities is unabashedly geared towards the number of such publications, it is not at all surprising to witness a decline in general scholarship over the years, and a consequent increase in the proportion of researchers. The age of occupationally rewarding specialized research has thus made genuine scholarship a somewhat scarcer commodity in our academic institutions, while the information overload has severely fragmented the community of scholars into a multitude of specialist camps.

The fate of the intellectual has become even more precarious than that of a pure scholar. With intellect itself under assault within the ramparts of academe, the intellectual has indeed become a fast vanishing breed today. Intellectuals may be distinguished by their interest in being informed by a wide range of disciplines as well as in obtaining a broad historical perspective and critical understanding of the knowledge enterprise in general. The intellectual orientation is typified by a primary interest in ideas, interpretation, criticism, commentary, synthesis, and search for meaning.

Like scholars engaged in research, academic intellectuals may engage in broad-based scholarly work which may have varying degrees of general, historical, philosophical, social or cultural significance – often going beyond the given boundaries of a discipline. Thus intellectuals essentially perform a critical-evaluative function both within and beyond their own disciplines. Popper's observation that the "great men of science were critical individuals"[12] is thus also applicable to intellectuals and great thinkers in general.

In this sense, all great thinkers whose ideas have changed the way we think about the natural world, and about society and human nature, have been primarily intellectual in their basic orientation to the knowledge enterprise – although they clearly form an incomparable category of their own, which is now rarely witnessed in academia. That many of these great thinkers expressed even such seminal ideas in characteristically unacademic language is a fact that needs to be specifically emphasized in an age of abstruse scholarly writing which is understood only by a handful of other select scholars. Woodring has expressed this point very candidly:

> Many scholars take pride in the fact that their publications can be read only by a select few. This posture is not limited to scientists; many avant garde critics write in a language that is meaningless to the general public and they, too, take pride in their unintelligibility. The fact remains that throughout the academic world, a clear and understandable literary style is referred to scornfully as "journalistic."
>
> The fact remains that some of the greatest books ever written contain little esoteric language and can be read and understood by any intelligent individual who has a modest background of liberal education. ... The fact that many of the "Great Books of the Western World" do not conform to the current academic standards of scholarly writing seems to suggest that there is a level of intellectual discourse that goes beyond and above what is commonly called scholarly writing ... painful as that fact may be to most academic[s].[13]

Only pedantic pretentiousness needs to be reinforced by abstruse jargon, out of a possible fear that "clear prose indicates an absence of thought" as Marshall McLuhan wryly observed.[14] Long ago, Nietzsche had also punctured such scholarly opaqueness with his typical aphoristic brilliance: "Those who know they are profound strive for clarity. Those who would like to seem profound to the crowd strive for obscurity."[15] Of course, such great and profound thinkers have been conspicuous by their absence for a good many years, which must lead us to wonder if the age of the great thinkers is over – just as the intellectual-scholar Northrop Frye had wondered "if the age of great writers or painters or composers is over… ."[16] There may be a lot of truth in what the great poet Walt Whitman said: "To have great poets, there must be great audiences, too."[17]

While we may wonder if Whitman's observation is also applicable in the case of great thinkers, there is no longer any need to wonder whether the age of the great thinkers is over. Almost undoubtedly, we have seen the last of the great thinkers in such universal intellectual giants as Darwin, Marx, William James, Nietzsche, Freud and Einstein, whose provocative and controversial ideas have challenged our views of humanity, society and the universe, and have continued to reverberate through the century – with no end in view. It is also highly unlikely that we will even see the likes of those outstanding intellects whose works have enriched the intellectual culture of our century – such exemplary minds as Bertrand Russell and Karl Popper, Aldous Huxley and George Orwell, Lewis Mumford and Lionel Trilling, Will Durant and Arnold Toynbee, Mortimer Adler and Jacques Barzun, Daniel Bell and David Riesman, John Kenneth Galbraith and E.F. Schumacher, Hannah Arendt and Jose Ortega y Gasset, Walter Kaufmann and Philip Rieff, Erich Fromm and Rollo May, Joseph Campbell and Alan Watts, Northrop Frye and Marshall McLuhan – to mention only a bare minimum of some of the more recognizable names in the relatively small pool of those whose writings have advanced our thought and knowledge in various fields of intellectual endeavor.

The intellectual landscape of our time would indeed have been a lot different and a lot poorer without the significant contributions of these and other such exceptional individuals to various areas of twentieth century intellectual thought. While their contributions may have varying life spans, albeit well into the future, many other current intellectual works in our relativistic age of competitive deconstructionism, may have a much shorter survival span. Perhaps it is time to recognize that even the age of such outstanding intellects may also be on the wane, even if it is not altogether over. We may well be running low on a great intellectual audience   which is not at all surprising given all the political and ideological distractions of a society that is also overloaded with information and entertainment on an unprecedented scale, to the point of leaving little time for reflective thought.

Be that as it may, what one may wonder and worry about now is how long an average intellectual can hold on in an academic fort besieged on all sides by the specialist forces. While the borders between researchers, scholars and intellectuals are permeable, the academic temper of our times has shown a perverse preference for a research-specialist mentality, which has proved fatal to liberal education and to the preservation of intellectual life in academia. This is all the more reason for an expeditious reform of higher education so that we may restore its prime focus on the cultivation of intellect via liberal education programs.

ʒ— IV —ᵫ

In such an academic climate it is not at all surprising that the art of teaching itself finally became a subject of scientific research and measurement – opening up an opportunity for those who had run out of ideas in their primary research areas. Evaluation and enhancement have thus acquired a dignity second only to research and development – proliferating in a similar fashion, largely in North American universities. Of course, administrative elation was inevitable now that the teaching evaluations could be used for purposes of weeding out the inefficient, enhancing the borderline, prodding the lazy, rewarding the worthy, and subduing the critics – or so it was believed. All this fervor seemed to suggest that teaching was fast becoming a dying art, and had to be enhanced in order to restore the public's waning confidence in the once impregnable institutions of higher learning. While the drunk in the story, even after having inundated his intellect, was at least looking for what he had lost – albeit not where it was lost but where there was more light, our academic administrators are not even looking for 'what' has been lost – let alone looking for it in the right place. So completely has the bureaucratization of education managed to suppress the 'what for?' in favor of the 'how to?' – with gimmicky teaching techniques for both the pedagogically challenged professors and the academically challenged students assuming far greater importance than the intellectual content and coherence of the curriculum.

The idea of student 'evaluation' of teaching performance obviously has some face validity, since it seems to give the appearance of having a necessary connection to the quality of teaching and education. Given the incontrovertible fact that the students have a right to be well-taught, and that the university has an obligation to provide good education, it is not surprising that the typical solutions proposed to eliminate bad teaching and promote good teaching are student evaluations and teaching enhancement/faculty development centers. However, it is important to note that such practices have proliferated largely in North American universities, where academics seem to have a relatively low immunity to all sorts of bandwagons that roll through the halls of academe. Critical thought is the only remedy for such academic epidemics.

That seemingly scientific solutions in this case rest on dubious assumptions is obvious from the fact that they have not been embraced by many academic institutions in other parts of the civilized world, not even by some of the most reputable institutions that provide excellent teaching and education. This in itself constitutes indubitable evidence that there is no necessary connection between good teaching and formal evaluations. Given such counter-examples, the teaching evaluation and enhancement hoopla begins to appear more like a red herring – thriving mainly on this side of the Atlantic. Parenthetically, we may also need to remind ourselves that the prototype of the university, Plato's Academy, had no teaching evaluations; the students then seem to have been more interested in enlightenment than in the formal evaluations of their enlighteners!

However, most teachers then and in yesteryears took up teaching as a calling, not simply as just another career like many of their modern counterparts. The former couldn't care less about evaluations, while the latter couldn't build a career without a portfolio of ratings. Moreover, since teaching is a cooperative art, like healing and farming, a learning context cannot really be evaluated properly without considering both parties in the situation, the teacher and the taught, at the same time. As everyone knows, a teacher can only help students learn, not make them learn, so that learning is a shared responsibility between teacher and student. While the teacher can only lead the student to the fount of knowledge, it is the student who is finally responsible for making the commitment to imbibe knowledge. Rationally speaking, then, it is only the evaluation of their joint contribution to learning which makes any sense.

It is obvious that the only two valid questions in student feedback are whether the teacher organized and taught the course in such a way that it promoted learning, and whether the student put in enough time, effort, reading and thought into learning. Everything else is mere commentary – so that the many research studies and standardized teaching evaluation forms are merely ways of keeping committees and experts busy, and in business.

Even a couple of examples would suffice to give some substance to our critical reflections on this subject. Two of the more frequent questions which appear on many standardized teaching evaluation forms have to do with whether the instructor presents carefully prepared and organized classes, and whether he/she shows a serious interest and enthusiasm in the subject and the teaching of it. On the face of it, these seem to be perfectly legitimate questions, but they turn out to be no more than skin deep.

With regard to the question of carefully prepared and organized classes, there can be no better counter-example than one who was recognized as one of the greatest teachers of all time, William James of Harvard University. James may not have scored enough for tenure or promotion on this one, since many times he was unorganized, full of 'ifs' and 'maybes', punctuated by "what was I just saying?" or "I can't think today" – not to mention a class-full of humorous anecdotes, and sometimes teaching philosophy during psychology classes, or vice versa. Of course, it would not have surprised or bothered James if the envious and the pretentious had called him a bad teacher in need of enhancement. Like all good teachers, James was always open to direct student feedback, but he had a definite aversion to what he called the "humbugging pretense of exactitude" – and would have so branded the many reliability and validity studies which make preposterous claims of exactitude in the measurement of teaching.

The question of the teacher displaying serious interest and enthusiasm in the subject and the teaching of it is equally problematic. That these qualities can be easily simulated was shown in the famous "Dr. Myron Fox" experiment, in which an actor mastered technical jargon and presented a nonsensical "scholarly" paper to a learned group of professionals – and received excellent evaluations for both presentation and subject matter even from accredited scholars holding doctoral degrees. Even after debriefing many found it very difficult to believe that they had been duped.[18] The moral for the learneds is more than obvious. To expect that students would be any more immune to such impression management than their mentors would only be two allow our hope to triumph over our experience. Moreover, given a choice, many would prefer the unenthusiastic digitally synthesized voice of a Stephen Hawking to that of an enthusiastic teacher such as "Professor" Myron Fox. Enthusiasm certainly helps, but not without substantial content which is capable of stimulating thought and imagination.

Likewise, the expectation in some evaluation forms, namely, that students should be able to rate on a five-point scale how thoroughly their professors know and understand their subject, borders on both the comic and the moronic. In order for students to be able to provide such a rating, they would have to know the subject thoroughly themselves – in which case they would not bother taking the course!

In fact, most questions on many of the evaluation forms produced by such academic busyness are so absurd or banal that if one had to rate such questions on a three-point scale, one would have to place them exactly halfway between silly and stupid. That such questions are being used in evaluation forms to identify, reward and promote good teaching is not only ludicrous, but downright hazardous to the future of good teaching and education. Excellence in teaching can be judged even by a couple of simple and direct questions, while much mediocrity can be easily elevated through the dubious statistics of such standardized evaluation forms. What James called the "humbugging pretense of exactitude" is certainly not a characteristic of intellect. Educational researchers seem to have gone astray by not heeding Aristotle's cautionary advice that an educated person only "looks for as much precision as the nature of the subject allows" and that "the same degree of accuracy should not be demanded in all inquiries."[19] Minimal reflection is sufficient to recognize the pretense of accuracy in the so-called measurement of the complex art of teaching.

Nevertheless, student opinions are important even if they are mere opinions, since the rise and fall of student motivation seems to be geared to their perceptions and feelings that they are learning and enjoying – even though enjoyment seems to correlate more highly with self-estimates of learning rather than with independent measures of actual learning reflected in objective and essay tests. Regardless of the question of validity and reliability of such opinions, therefore, it is extremely important to be responsive to student feedback, for without motivation the students will neither listen nor learn.

However, accepting this fact of responsiveness to student concerns and problems, which is made possible on the basis of student feedback, does not imply the use of elaborate or standardized evaluation techniques. While some degree of standardization may well be possible in evaluating the training that is provided in some tangible areas of Science and in most Professional Studies, one must not presume that this is equally possible in the teaching of all disciplines. However, given the multi-ideological context of our modern university, combined with the subject matter of the Humanities and the Social Sciences, it is almost impossible to standardize the variations in teaching practices generated by the wide variations in content and in philosophical/educational backgrounds, objectives and goals – both between and within disciplines. It is equally impossible for such variations to be fairly represented and reflected in any standardized series of items, let alone evaluated on pseudo-quantitative rating scales, or mismeasured in terms of statistical stupidities such as averaged perceptions or percentage opinions used in political popularity polls. Much of the opposition to such teaching evaluations has therefore come from some of the best teachers and scholars in the Humanities and the Social Sciences – precisely because they have not succumbed to such scientism which trivializes teaching.

Indeed, there are variations in teaching styles and methods, as there are differences between student aptitudes and preferences. But the goals of education may be reached in many ways – even more so in the present multiversity system. It takes all kinds of teachers to make a university, as Jacques Barzun of Columbia University said almost half a century ago:

> It is extraordinary how many diverse kinds of men and women make desirable teachers … . Remember you need lecturers and discussers and tutors. They can differ in endless, unpredictable ways. You can take the halt, the lame, the blind; men with speech defects or men who cannot be heard above a whisper; … men who are lazy and slow, who are bright and unstable, or incorrigible enfants terribles; you can risk some who are deficient in learning, and join them to form an admirable as well as an induplicable faculty. This is possible because the students also display a variety of human traits that cannot all be reached and moved by the same spells.[20]

Given such a bewildering variety of people who can make up a decent faculty, we need to become a little more realistic about this business of standardized forms of teaching evaluation – lest we become so enhanced and entranced by the perfection of means that we lose sight of our ends.

Yet, it is both understandable and fair that students would like to exercise some control over their learning situation, even if not over their professors – although it is a well known fact that teaching evaluations often become one way for students to ensure that they would at least get good grades, if not a good education. However, without ensuring student awareness of learning as a joint responsibility shared by both teacher and student, we can never be sure if what pupil Paul says about Professor Peter in his evaluation tells us more about pupil Paul or Professor Peter.

Moreover, the potential for anonymity to become irresponsibility is an even more legitimate concern in an atmosphere of political correctness, and conflicting ideological interests – not to mention possibly latent racial and ethnic biases. Like peer evaluation in such a milieu, student evaluations may also have a potential for penalizing those on the wrong side of the political, ideological and racial-ethnic fences – especially in the humanities and social sciences, which deal with many controversial issues. Such evaluations also have a clear potential for abuse in the hands of disgruntled and non-serious students – even when they have not been explicitly influenced by their ideological-political affiliations. Unfortunately, anonymous computer-friendly evaluation forms and statistics do not differentiate between responses from serious or slack students.

If the real purpose of student 'evaluation' of teaching is feedback and enhancement so that teachers can help students learn more effectively, then an end of the semester evaluation is too late – since it cannot retroactively help the students who have already completed the course. Such a predicament can only be avoided by encouraging students to provide periodic feedback to professors, even as often as after each class in the form of questions, concerns and comments directly or through an in-class student representative. Without such mutual trust between the teacher and the taught, especially in the give and take of liberal learning, evaluation techniques can have a detrimental effect on educational standards as professors try to accommodate courses to the wishes of the students for the sake of good evaluations. When students study only for the sake of exams and grades, rather than learn for the sake of learning, they may do immense harm to their education. Likewise, when professors teach for the sake of getting good evaluations rather than for increasing the scholarship level of students, they can corrupt the whole purpose of higher education.

In any case, if past experience and present trends are any indication, then one may expect that by the time the students realize that such banal quick-fixes cannot really enhance their educational experience, a new and improved bureaucratic whitewash will be made available to them by ingenious educational researchers and popularity conscious administrators who are ever busy covering up our confusion of goals by conjuring up even more innovative techniques and gimmicks to distract students from the real issues. Meanwhile, amidst all this apparent pedagogical progress, we move even further away from ensuring the provision of meaningful and wholesome liberal education programs at the undergraduate level.

◌— V —◌

As in the case of many other issues in academic institutions, the whole confusion on this subject of teaching evaluation and enhancement seems to result from a lack of semantic clarification on two fronts. First, it is important to note the confusion in the basic terminology employed by most educational researchers and academics. Strictly speaking, terms such as 'evaluation' and 'rating' imply certain standards in the assigning of value to an object, event, person or performance. Evaluations may be expressed either in terms of quantitative judgements based on standardized measurements using calibrated instruments and scales, or in terms of qualitative judgements based on accepted criteria which may be academic, aesthetic, rational, legal, social or moral. Obviously, then, evaluations and ratings have to be based on a knowledge and understanding of accepted standards, and on experience and skill in making judgements.

However much it may be dressed up to look scientifically respectable, student feedback simply cannot qualify as evaluation in this sense, since it involves essentially different elements: subjective opinions based on global impressionistic judgements involving individual perceptions and feelings, which are not based on generally accepted standards of measurement or judgement. Of course, neither experience nor skill are needed when it comes to giving such subjectively based opinions. No better proof is needed to show the anti-intellectual climate in academia than this whole farcical process of assigning numerical values to subjective impressions, adding these up as if they represented true measures, and then finding an average value to represent the quality of teaching – even without having defined either 'quality' or 'teaching' in the first place. Such pseudo-measurement would be no different from a process of obtaining the weight of an individual by averaging the readings from a large number of uncalibrated scales, and then using such average measures to determine and compare weight loss or weight gain after different diet programs. Humbug is no less humbug even if it appears in a scientific guise.

On the second front, there is an even more ingrained confusion. Both dictionary meaning and usage make teaching synonymous with instruction, but the art of teaching must not be equated with the science of instruction as we need two distinct pedagogical labels to uphold our earlier distinction between education and training. Ideally speaking, education refers to the process of gradual awakening of the mind by cultivation of intellect through teaching and critical examination of seminal ideas of humanity which provide food for reflective thought. On the other hand, by definition, training is aimed at promoting specific skills and abilities by providing systematic instruction and discipline in which information, rules, and techniques play the critical role. Instruction of the sort that is given in professional studies and vocational institutions is necessarily based on a clear set of objectives which may be achieved in varying degrees, and in defined periods of time, given student cooperation. The learning that takes place under such conditions is more easily attributable to the specific design of the training program. Instruction can therefore be subjected to realistic evaluation in terms of approximation to the objectives set forth.

However, teaching is an open ended activity with long range goals, since education itself is a life-long process. Education is never completed in college or university; in fact very few are meaningfully educated even after a doctoral degree. Real education often begins only after completion of the academic formalities, provided that teaching has fostered in the students a love of learning and an appreciation of a variety of great ideas in the intellectual tradition. Teaching thus inculcates the habits of the mind represented by the liberating arts of reading, writing, reflecting, reasoning, judging, and critical thinking.

Unlike instruction, teaching in this sense is geared towards education rather than training, which means towards examining significant ideas and raising disturbing questions, rather than simply acquiring information or developing skills useful in a given occupation. While teaching and instruction may share the requirements of commitment and communication, good teaching in a liberal arts program requires not only a broad mastery of ideas in one's own discipline, but at least some familiarity with significant ideas in many other disciplines. The implication here is that teaching is inherently generalist, and even Socratically subversive, in contrast to the inherently specialist, standardized and conformist nature of instruction.

Such teaching then cannot be so easily subjected to measurement and evaluation – especially in the context of a liberal education program which is committed to intangible long-term goals like "love of learning" and "love of ideas" and to the cultivation of the powers of critical reflection and judgement. It is sheer folly even to expect that approximations to such intangible goals can be recognized clearly enough by students, let alone explicitly evaluated or measured on standardized forms at the end of any single course after each twelve to fifteen week long semester.

The mystique of measurement and methodology has such a potent grip on academic imagination in North America that anyone seriously questioning it is branded as a reactionary belonging to an old and outmoded school of thought. However, it is such cult-like veneration of scientific evaluation techniques which has kept the educational experts gainfully employed, not only in promoting the measurement of teaching but, ipso facto, in the business of promoting various methodologies of teaching – whereby they have degraded the art of teaching into a technology of instruction.

In fact, the really great teachers are identified more by the general qualities of personality, rather than by the types of methodology – as is obvious from the fact that we remember teachers, not their techniques. Yet we try to use methods to mimic their performance, as Margaret Mead notes: "The most extraordinary thing about a really good teacher is that he or she transcends accepted educational methods. Such methods are designed to help average teachers approximate the performance of good teachers."[21]

The current popularity of methodologies must therefore mean that we either have an abundance of mediocre teachers who must learn instructional methods, or that we do not distinguish sufficiently between instruction for purposes of training, and teaching for purposes of education. While methodologies may improve instruction, no method has yet been devised to transform average teachers into really good teachers for purposes of higher education. As Peter Drucker observed: "In teaching we rely on the 'naturals,' the ones who somehow know how to teach"[22] – because they have, in addition to a good grasp of knowledge, such natural qualities like passion and commitment to learning and education, whereby they are able to get themselves and their willing and able students caught up in a world of ideas and thought. No method can mimic such passion, dedication, knowledge and understanding.

The illusion that technique is more important than content has been the bane of North American universities. The 'seminar' is a good example of both good technique and good intentions gone awry. Introduced by Woodrow Wilson, soon after he assumed presidency of Princeton University in 1902, the "preceptorial" system, as it was then called, emphasized guided individualized dialogue and discussion between faculty and students instead of the more one-way lecture system. For the highly motivated students interested in ideas, reading, thinking and discussing, such tutorial sessions, preceded and followed by well thought-out and critically focused lectures, are an ideal combination in a well-structured and knowledge-based liberal studies program.

However, such educative seminars seem to have played right into the hands of professors dedicated to the ideal of an easy life, or to the more ambitious goal of career building through research, committee work and campus politics. Reducing their workload through rap sessions was an ideal way for professors to pose as progressive-democratic teachers – with pious proclamations that they were simply abdicating their status as authority figures. Of course, such self-righteous gestures are based on the common confusion between authoritarian power and the intellectual authority of the teacher which comes from greater knowledge, understanding and experience. Only such a distinction enables us to appreciate Thomas Szasz's judgement that "a teacher should have maximal authority, and minimal power."[23]

Yet, the self-acclaimed non-authorities do not hesitate to act as wise moderators and facilitators of the free-floating exchanges of mere opinion, ideology or ignorance between relatively unmotivated, unprepared, uncritical or uninformed students. Paradoxically, the appearance of freedom can also become a perfect form of subjugation, à la Rousseau, since it increases the potential risk of independent and critical thought becoming compromised by subtle forms of selective reinforcement, ideological manipulation and group-think made possible by the dynamics of prof and peer pressure, especially in opinion-based courses relating to social-political issues and policies. At best, then, such infertile round-table seminars can only promote professorial pretense of piety, which is impressive enough to create in relatively uninformed students the impression of an enjoyable learning-cum-growth experience – albeit one that does not generate any real growth in knowledge, understanding or wisdom. Thus, in this context, it may be best to heed William Blake's admonition: "Go! put off Holiness, and put on Intellect."[24]

Such academic gamesmanship has not gone unnoticed within the academe itself. While graduate seminars may be somewhat more productive than their undergraduate counterparts, Pierre van den Berghe still thought it necessary to make some caustic comments in the form of advice to academics:

> A graduate seminar in your field requires little if any preparation at all. You just distribute a reading list, assign topics to your students, let them do most of the talking, and confine your activities to two or three wise remarks a week.[25]

Thus, a great deal of gimmickry has become standard under euphemisms such as "innovative teaching techniques" and "student-centered learning" – which may often leave many a modern student happier, if not any wiser. Teaching has indeed become, as Mark Twain once observed, "the fine art of imparting knowledge, without possessing it!" All such trends may eventually culminate in electronic universities – with all progressive flesh and blood professors replaced by the full learner-centered technology of the internet.

⟿ VI ⟾

If the primary focus of education is to be on the 'what' rather than the 'how', then teaching little or useless content very well cannot serve the aims of higher education. What is not worth teaching is not worth teaching well, which means at least half of what is included in the undergraduate curriculums of most university programs. Given the diversity of faculty and student interests, plus the many popular and politically correct fashions of the day, and an essentially cafeteria-style elective system, it has become imperative to focus on the 'what' in the curriculum – even to maintain a minimal level of higher education. The proliferation of academic courses has resulted in a cafeteria-cum-supermarket atmosphere in the universities, as Herbert London observed:

> There are courses that are hard and courses that are soft; there are some which pander to race and gender and others bereft of any meaning; there are some with value and others that are translations of "Sesame Street" for immature adolescents. As the university's purpose becomes increasingly ambiguous, catalogues get thicker. Not only is there a college for everyone, now there is a course for everyone. Instead of reading texts which liberate the individual from a narrow, provincial, limited perspective, avatars of a new culture argue for those texts which reinforce the study of what is familiar or what passes for political acceptability.[26]

Ironically, it is in the rhetoric of ideologically-based courses and in the jargon of methodology-based specialized courses that obscurity is often confused with profundity and gimmickry with discovery. On the other hand, the deep insights stated simply in the works of great thinkers are obliviously dismissed as simplistic or dated. Needless to add that all this pseudo-sophistication cannot but be conducive to the production of methodologically dense or ideologically muddled minds. Academic programs which promote so much pedantry and ideology under the guise of knowledge must obviously contribute more to the sum total of stupidity than to the enhancement of wisdom. Higher education thus continues to lose the academic battle as more and more universities commit themselves to producing pretentious pedants, semi-literate researchers, technicians and ideologues – instead of scholars, intellectuals and enlightened citizens.

In the modern academic supermarket students have few guideposts – except for some rather pompous mission statements in university catalogues – their pomposity being inversely related to reality. Neither faculty nor administrators seem to mind such serious discrepancies between image and reality, while the student advisory system provides the necessary whitewash to cover up the confusion in the curriculum, which any thoughtful student must inevitably experience. Thus the primary blame for the absence of guidance for students seeking a good education may be placed on both administrators and faculty, as Robert Proctor has well observed:

> They [administrators and faculty] themselves have no coherent philosophy of education. They have few, if any, intellectual interests outside of their own academic specialty. They accept uncritically the fragmentation of the college and high school curriculum as somehow reflecting the nature of knowledge itself. They have neither the desire to think deeply and seriously about the nature and purpose of education, nor the historical consciousness such thinking demands. They suffer, in short, from the same intellectual fragmentation and cultural amnesia that afflicts our students. Such teachers and administrators are embarrassed by student demands for serious intellectual guidance, because they are unable to give it. So they pass the buck – to the students and their parents.[27]

The current disillusionment of students with higher education cannot therefore be alleviated by teaching evaluations and the development of ever new teaching techniques, but by proper guidance, and by the enrichment of the intellectual content of the curriculum. Equally important is genuine professorial commitment to teaching, not the kind which, like the counterfeit seminars, is compatible with careerism, lucrative consulting and campus politics. Of course, nothing ties up the real business of education as all the wasteful and counterproductive committee work – which, as Veblen had observed, was "designed chiefly to keep the faculty talking while the bureaucratic machine goes on its way under the guidance of the executive and his [her] personal counsellors and lieutenants."[28]

∽— VII —∾

However, all the president's men and women cannot put higher education back together again even with their total quality bureaucratic management. In fact, academic bureaucracy is the primary source of politicization and polarization in the university. While governments and societies have always imposed demands and restrictions on universities, and burdened them with educational irrelevancies, it is the administration that serves like an official Trojan horse for the internal assault on the community of scholars. The "peculiar disease of Administration", Paul Goodman noted, "is that it replaces, in a formal and functionless way, the community of scholars itself. It is able not only to lodge in the college, but to take it over and make it hardly indistinguishable from the extramural world."[29] Amazingly, all this is done in a judo-like fashion by utilizing the resources of ambitious academics who are only too happy to please the administration.

Major academic committees can often be covertly rigged up by a clever administration to provide an illusion of decentralized decision-making. Of course, co-opted faculty members on compromised committees, dazed by such an honor, become committed to voting at their party's call and not thinking for themselves at all – thereby surreptitiously increasing bureaucratic control over fellow faculty members by passing petty policies that usually cannot even pass the basic test of reasonableness. However, administrative decisions are generally rationalized in terms of committee recommendations, rather than being justified by rational arguments. More often than not, therefore, presidential visions promulgated when taking office soon become blurred by academic astigmatism, and thus distort the focus on the main purpose of higher education.

Perhaps, we need to reconsider what Veblen believed to be the only remedial measure for the rehabilitation of higher learning: "All that is required is the abolition of the academic executive and the governing board. Anything short of this heroic remedy is bound to fail, because the evils sought to be remedied are inherent in these organs, and intrinsic to their functioning."[30] In these times of tight funding for universities, it makes a great deal of sense to ask why administrators should be paid such high salaries when the basic mission of a university is teaching and scholarship. Veblen's proposal for removing the two chief obstacles in the institutions of higher learning may therefore be the kindest cut of all – reducing the exorbitant cost of running the presidential office, and restoring the ideals of higher education without any hindrance from government-dominated and market-oriented governing boards. With all the knowledge and expertise present in today's universities, self-governing colleges or communities of scholars, assisted by the essential support services, can be a far more economical and effective alternative for providing all the functions of these offices, namely, graceful speeches on ceremonial occasions, fund-raising and public-relations. Of course, the last two of these functions are now delegated by many universities to special offices and professional consultants. While university presidents have never suffered from the fear of flying to exotic destinations for the stated purpose of building educational bridges and searching for prospective students, even such practices no longer seem cost-effective, given the immense advertising power of the world-wide-web internet technology.

Yet, even the self-governing alternative is not without its own problems. The ubiquity of the politically ambitious institutional academic and the faculty ideologue constitutes the gravest danger to fostering intellectual life in universities, regardless of the type of academic governance. That the community of scholars is no longer bound by an intellectual tradition of critical thought is obvious from the fact that so many academics unquestioningly succumb to political and ideological agendas concealed under the pious cover of program enrichment, as they unwittingly allow themselves to be manipulated by a cleverly managed and manufactured consensus of opinion – even on issues which require reflective thought and rational judgement. Thus, with such self-serving academics in charge of the system it may not be any easier to create a milieu conducive to enhancing the intellectual climate or to promoting genuine creative scholarship.

Eric Hoffer's penetrating analysis of the underlying dynamics of this apparent paradox of "intellectual" power in the larger social context seems equally applicable to our academic context:

> The reason for this is to be found in the role of the noncreative pseudo-intellectual in such a system. The genuinely creative person lacks, as a rule, the temperament requisite for the seizure, the exercise, and, above all, the retention of power. Hence, when the intellectuals come into their own, it is usually the pseudo-intellectual who rules the roost,

and he is likely to imprint his mediocrity and meagerness on every phase of cultural activity. Moreover, his creative impotence brews in him a murderous hatred of intellectual brilliance, and he may be tempted ... to enforce a crude levelling of all intellectual activity.[31]

According to Hoffer, people mind their own business when it is worth minding – as would be the case with most creative scholars and genuine intellectuals. On the other hand, the power-cum-envy driven institutional academics are more like Hoffer's true believers, who like to mind other people's business in order to take their mind off either their own trifling affairs or their own meager intellectual aptitude. As a consequence of the bureaucratic maneuverings of such zealous academics, who have the mentality of totalitarian commissars, the academic atmosphere becomes polluted by piddling policies and the politics of power-mongering – and is therefore unable to sustain a shared intellectual tradition. A community of scholars committed to preserving its intellectual heritage thus gives way to a collective of academics diversely dedicated to the self-serving pursuit of power and to the expansion of the curriculum to include all the currently fashionable and politically correct ideologies. While one may agree with Edward Said that the university "still can offer the intellectual a quasi-utopian space" for reflection and scholarship,[32] these new pressures and constraints threaten to further shrink whatever remaining space does exist.

The dilemmas of governance may not be resolvable until the university itself is fully transformed from an academic technocracy into a full-time learning society, diligently dedicated to the cause of higher education. Any kind of transforming experience for the students that would generate a sense of intellectual growth or a genuine sense of becoming educated can be brought about only when academic policies are guided by the intellectual ideals of higher education, rather than by the bookkeeping mentality of self-glorifying administrators who are guided solely by the bureaucratic ideals of efficiency and visibility, and the corporate ideals of cost-effective productivity. Since a bureaucratic-cum-corporate mentality has become a job-related requirement for all administrative offices, the only remedy for freeing the grip of such a mentality on higher education would seem to lie in exhorting academic administrators to fulfill their talents by moving into fields such as government, business, industry or the army.

While ideological deconstruction of the curriculum in recent years has adulterated scholarship and degraded the intellect, the onus for the malaise of higher education must also rest, to a great extent, on the power and prevalence of the public-or-perish philosophy of productivity that has been in vogue for so long. In fact, one may also surmise that the deconstructonist agenda itself may be the unwholesome fruit of such a pernicious philosophy – if we may judge by the sheer increase in productivity of papers and "texts" which can mean anything or nothing.

Not surprisingly, there is an incompatibility in this business of academic publications which is rarely admitted in public, even when it is tacitly acknowledged within scholarly circles. Quantity and quality are often at odds with each other whenever extrinsic pressures are paramount. While felicitations may or may not follow publication, speedy publications clearly have more than a survival value since academic status is firmly tied to the sheer number of publications. Evidently, such an emphasis on quantity discourages original works of scholarship which cannot be generated rapidly, or according to preset publication quotas. Thus it is the bureaucratically motivated practices and priorities, including a misguided notion of accountability, which have contributed in large measure to dampening faculty enthusiasm for broadening scholarship through study of some of the great works of humanity and some of the significant contributions of modern scholars. As award-winning scholar Page Smith also observes: "The best and only research that should be expected of university professors is wide and informed reading in their fields and in related fields." This is not only "real research," he notes, but the only kind which enhances teaching: "The best teachers are almost invariably the most widely informed, those with the greatest range of interests and most cultivated minds."[33]

In fact, such a generalist approach, with primary emphasis on study, understanding and synthesis of significant ideas, can have a far greater impact on undergraduate teaching than specialized research and esoteric publications which happen to be the order of the day. The slogan that teaching and such abstruse research complement one another, so that one cannot do a good job of one without the other, thus turns out to be no more than another sacred cow of academia – which needs to be driven out of the groves of academe. Barzun's critique of such an ill-conceived philosophy about four decades ago is still the most relevant:

Defenders of the system as it is often say that good teaching is inseparable from research and that the man who ceases studying at twenty-five is a dried out and dull teacher ten years later. These are two statements that only seem to be the same. Of course the teacher must keep reading and thinking abreast of his time, but this does not mean that he must write and publish. The confusion hides a further absurd assumption, which is that when a man writes a scholarly book that reaches a dozen specialists he adds immeasurably to the world's knowledge; whereas if he imparts his thought and his reading to one hundred and fifty students every year, he is wasting his time and leaving the world in darkness. One is tempted to ask what blinkered pedant ever launched the notion that students in coming to college secede from the human race and may therefore be safely left out when knowledge is being broadcast.[34]

Given such a state of affairs, it is not at all difficult to guess why universities are so much more enthusiastic about faculty research and productivity than about student education – ironically in the name of higher education. As one philosopher put it, albeit in an altogether different academic context, all this is so preposterously silly that only very learned people could have thought of institutionalizing such a philosophy.

There is little hope for the survival of liberal education in universities which are turned into a hodgepodge of research-development institutes, teaching-enhancement centers, socialization schools, political camps, ideological battlefields, and conflict-resolution clinics for gender, racial and other disputes. With such a medley of academically irrelevant and disconnected aims, combined with collectivist thinking, a fragmented curriculum, and multiple specialisms, an intellectual community of scholars has indeed become a relic of the past, while intellect itself has been placed in jeopardy.

Chapter V

* *

The Malady of the
Academic Knowledge Industry

*Except to intellect itself, there is no risk involved in the new academic
productivity.*

- Philip Rieff
Fellow Teachers[1]

T he incisive brevity and the apparent nonchalance of Rieff's astute
observation must not keep us from a candid and searching
examination of the academic context which has given rise to such a
puzzling and paradoxical development.

With the growing responsiveness of the academic community to the
immediate needs of society over the last half century, it was inevitable
that the university would finally become transformed into a knowledge
industry – infiltrated by the philosophy and practices of business and
economics. Thus, when the idea of mass production of knowledge
captured the scholarly imagination, academic institutions became
transformed into research-publication factories and operated on an
assembly-line model. What one may call the "Gutenberg Mania" thus
became the most fashionable epidemic in academia – promoting pedantic
productivity at the expense of genuine creativity and scholarship.

Research & Development, or R & D as it is lovingly called, was the
Trojan horse which industry placed inside the gates of the universities
soon after the Second World War, and pushed even deeper into the
halls of learning after the Sputnik about a decade later. Since then
academics as well as administrators have literally prostrated themselves
before this high profile dummy. Thus the belief that most research
carried out in universities is worthwhile became the supreme sacred

cow of academia – sustaining and enhancing many academic careers over the years.

While R & D is perfectly legitimate for industry, and just as important for the country as education, it cannot be made into the centerpiece of an educational institution without causing some adverse side effects. In fact, some intellectuals and scholars, like Rieff, have even questioned the very presence of R & D in universities, believing that it is actually contributing to the destruction of our universities.

Unlike scholarship, which is at the very heart of higher learning, the notion of R & D only enhances the crass commercialization of knowledge to the point where lucrative business contracts and a profit-oriented obsession with productivity perverts the disinterested pursuit of truth. Almost insidiously, the intellectual-scholarly quest for knowledge has been adulterated by the business philosophy of 'research and development' – which allows marketable ideas to enter the competitive economy as marketable goods, and to sway in and out of fashion in the same way.

However, confusing productivity with creativity promotes a great deal of mediocrity in both goods and ideas. Subsidized or forced productivity in the humanities and social sciences leads to even more disastrous consequences by further narrowing the boundaries of thought from disciplines into sub-specialisms. Nonetheless, marketability has continued to guide research and discovery – only to feed them into an already runaway technology, while development as measured by progress in technology has prevailed as the prime economic index of GNP. Large scale research has become more fashionable – just as everything big was beautiful in the pre-Schumacher era. "The spirit of science has changed as a result of organized research," Popper noted with concern, warning that "the enormous new organizations of scientific research represent a serious danger to science."[2]

The science industry is now a vast collective institution of highly specialized fields in which problems are pre-defined for teams of budding scientists on the basis of the current stage of various research projects. On such a collective assembly-line, the individual scientist is merely an efficient but replaceable entity, not an indispensable creative mind. As Erich Kahler puts it, "It is the project, the design that counts. Who does the work is often relatively unimportant."[3] Thus the highly individual nature of the scientific quest witnessed among the great thinkers of the past cannot but wane in the teamwork of collective science –

notwithstanding the likes of such brilliant individual minds as Stephen Hawking, David Bohm, Richard Feynman, and Ilya Prigogine.

The symbiotic relationship of research with industry contributes a great deal to the prosperity of the university – even as it gives it an appearance of an assembly-line factory. Institutions of higher learning now have to be run like business enterprises, so that corporate thinking promotes productivity and profit as the crucial measures for judging the very health and survival of academic programs and people. Researchers keep busy scratching much trivia to a tune set by the new academic managers, whose talents are often more suitable for assembly-line plants than for the halls of intellect. Einstein's ticklish epigram "you can't scratch if you don't itch"[4] has remained unheeded – not counting displays of merely pretentious academic itching, and jargonized displays of knowledge to cover up the underlying ignorance. It was precisely in order to avoid the pressures of a 'publish-or-perish' philosophy, which generally leads to superficial results, that Einstein had even urged scientists and scholars to find non-demanding jobs (like that of a cobbler!) for the purposes of earning their living. "Only when we do not have to be accountable to anybody," said Einstein, "can we find joy in the scientific endeavor."[5]

The increasing dependence of universities on government funding over the years has promoted the bureaucratization of knowledge and the demand for accountability – with productivity and efficiency becoming the chief indicators of academic performance. A single R representing research has thus come to pose a potent threat to the three traditional R's of higher education – reading, reflection and 'riting. Paper-shuffling has literally become the hallmark in such an academic environment of explicitly external expectations and monetary incentives. The unavoidable consequence of all this is the constant churning out of anything printable, however frivolous, fragmented or fabricated – while thoughtful and enduring scholarly or intellectual works of broad scope and significance fade into obscurity.

Paradoxically, then, the increasingly fashionable slogan of accountability may actually be as hazardous to the future of higher education, as were the earlier increases in funding which irrevocably impaired its central purpose through a proliferation of anti-intellectual programs. External accountability to administrators, governing boards and funding agencies not only promotes an outward show of much wasteful work to pad up academic resumes, but facilitates a pitiful conformity to the politically correct or fundable fashions of the day. In this process of ingratiating oneself to the powers that be, academic freedom itself is eroded to an extent that the critical function of the academic is wasted away in the complacency of specialized research – which, like committee work, superficially satisfies the requirements of accountability, but is equally counterproductive for purposes of higher education. On the other hand, a genuine sense of responsibility, love of learning, and dedication to the intellectual ideals of higher education are critical for purposes of enhancing knowledge, understanding, and wisdom – one's own and that of one's students. In the spirit of Einstein, therefore, we may also say that only when we do not have to be accountable to anybody can we find true joy in the academic endeavors of teaching and scholarship.

Bureaucratization and commercialization of knowledge thus encourage salesmanship rather than scholarship by creating an environment of free-floating grants – available to all those willing to play the game of grantsmanship, which basically involves a proper packaging of proposals on timely topics favored by the granting agencies. Such a subsidized academic climate, in which the potential enduring value of research and scholarship has become a negligible consideration, creates a great deal of wasteful gimmickry. This is all too obvious from the fact that speedy obsolescence is the characteristic fate of much of current research – as it is of most commercial products in a culture of consumption. Likewise, much of research is neither consumed nor ever exhumed – and becomes the academic equivalent of dust-collecting junk in many a home basement. Rieff's concern is therefore very pertinent in this context:

> Why publish? That is the real question for all scholars of meanings; for all intellectuals, as well. The world is broken through enough. With so many authors, who remains behind to read? Every man his own original: that is democracy sold out, and an impossible culture.[6]

A publish-or-perish philosophy which dictates that everyone must publish, in the long run, corrupts both writing and thinking. One obvious outcome of this is pedantic pretentiousness reinforced by abstruse jargon – comparable to the near incomprehensible officialese of bureaucratic communication. While such cultivated obscurity has enabled many academics to prosper, what seems to have perished in the process is thought itself.

Moreover, it is often the case that a piece of research is obsolete even before it sees the light of print in a journal. Even though much of academic research seems to thus fade into obscurity faster than the time it took to fill out grant applications and do the study, the researcher has nevertheless got a paper or two out of it. Such papers may even be presented at various conferences, where discussions that follow may be as trite as the jargon-loaded dissertations. While most of these conference papers do not really contribute to the advancement of knowledge, most academic conferences do boost the business of bars, restaurants, hotels and other tourist attractions in the cities where the conferences are held. Thus economic gains far outweigh gains in knowledge. Nevertheless, one can report such papers on the updated resume before passing it on to the Dean to be filed in electronic storage – perhaps for the amusement of posterity. It is doubtful though that posterity will be much amused by all this academic gobbledygook – even if, perchance, it ever found time to wade through this information glut while surfing on the academic internet.

Many eminent scholars of the day have also realized that publishing is chiefly serving the ends of perfunctory accountability, professional competition and pecuniary rewards. Any genuine concern with knowledge fades into the background when the drive for knowledge succumbs to career advancement. The competitive philosophy endemic in a business culture has to a great extent displaced the disinterested pursuit of truth – which, however, continues to receive lip-service in the art of grantsmanship. Of course, the bureaucratically minded academic managers have been instrumental in reinforcing this transformation with their stick-and-carrot tactics – which are more suitable for rabbits than for academics.

A possible remedy for all this would have been to follow the ingenious suggestion of a Berkeley University scholar, David Daube, to the effect that everyone be appointed at first to full-professorship, and then receive demotions and proportionate reductions in salary for each publication.[7] If such a system had been adopted, we may be sure that the academic knowledge industry would have come to a screeching halt. It is anybody's guess as to how many Galileos would then have been willing to risk their livelihood for a few measly words like "and yet it moves."

As we know, this would have been an interesting scenario, albeit too good to be true in the real world of academia. Getting to the top of the academic totem-pole has long been a top-priority game among career-minded scholars. In this topsy-turvy academic world, vagueness has often passed for depth, and jargon for originality. To add insult to injury, unintelligibility has been promoted as 'scholarship' but clarity denounced as 'journalistic' – with typical academic amnesia for the supreme clarity of many of the works of the great intellects of humanity. Alice would have been equally puzzled in this academic wonderland!

Almost like colonies of rabbits, journals, papers and researchers have all multiplied exponentially over the years – only knowledge has not kept pace with this long march of academic productivity. It is almost as if Gresham's law has operated with a vengeance, since the sheer quantity of research has literally driven out ideas of quality. The disastrous consequences of this were placed in sharp relief by Lewis Mumford:

> Though this program for the automatic mass production of knowledge originated in science, ... it has been imitated in the humanities, particularly in American universities, as a sort of status symbol, to underwrite budget requests in competition with the physical and social sciences, and to provide a quantitative measure for professional promotions. Whatever the original breach between the sciences and the humanities, in method they have now – pace Charles Snow! – become one. Though they run different assembly lines, they belong to the same factory. The mark of their common deficiency is that neither has given any serious consideration to the results of their uncontrolled automation. ... Meanwhile, a vast amount of valuable knowledge becomes relegated, along with an even greater amount of triviality and trash, to a mountainous rubbish heap.[8]

Operating thus on a factory model, most universities have trained and cloned highly efficient assembly-line technicians, who operate under the illusion that mass production of information is an intrinsic good for humanity – although, ironically, the inevitable consequence of all this over time was the devaluation of the humanities. Cultivation of the mind through the use of reflective thought and imaginative experience becomes less and less important as the temple of intellect continues to be eroded by such factory-minded money-changers of our times.

꩜— II —꩜

While we have rightly concerned ourselves with the adverse biological and environmental side-effects resulting from the industrial pollution of our atmosphere and biosphere, we have ignored the mind-numbing effects resulting from the information pollution of our 'noosphere' (the "thinking envelope of the earth")[9] caused by a couple of million publications annually. Whether this is progress or madness may no longer be debatable, since such high levels of information cannot but produce noise and confusion. Gresham's law seems to apply equally well in the realm of knowledge: bad ideas drive away good ideas, or at least they make their discrimination more difficult – since the good, the bad, and the trivial all get piled up in what Mumford called a "mountainous rubbish heap." Moreover, when quality becomes difficult even to recognize, let alone evaluate, quantitative criteria become the hallmark of progress.

An almost cancerous increase of information may well be called 'Parkinson's malady' – an unhealthy expansion of information that pollutes the noosphere and endangers the intellect. "Excessive increase of anything," as Plato had said, "often causes a reaction in the opposite direction." Accordingly, in keeping with the law of entropy, it would not be too far-fetched to assume that such surplus information, too, would quickly degenerate into noise. Information overload degenerates into noise despite technological facilities like electronic storage. As a matter of fact such facilities actually aggravate the information pollution much as "widening a traffic artery in a city," according to Mumford, "actually increases the amount of traffic" and intensifies congestion.[10] The hazards of the information superhighway may thus be far more serious than even the casualties that occur daily on the automobile expressways.

Parkinson's Law thus operates with as much force in the knowledge industry as in a bureaucracy, so that research expands to consume all the academic time, journal space and public funds available – much of it to no avail. Rifkin's observation is to the point: "As more and more information is beamed at us, less and less of it can be absorbed, retained, and exploited." All the bits and bytes of information can bite into the very core of intellect, so that even the capacity to make rational judgements can become seriously impaired when one is assailed by such massive doses of disconnected information from all sides. A high rate of expansion in the 'noisphere' may therefore be regarded as a potent threat to the survival of intellect in society.

The information explosion, and the consequent fallout in the form of specialisms, have already become hazardous for the survival of liberal education. However inevitable may be the trend towards the mass production of knowledge, and however out of control the cancerous increase in information, the story of the child in Andersen's tale may have a message for us. Many academic emperors, too, are almost naked – despite the opaqueness of their paper-thin academic robes which barely conceal the pedantic pretentiousness underneath. As Stanislav Andreski observed:

> What is particularly dismaying is that not only does the flood of publications reveal an abundance of pompous bluff and a paucity of new ideas, but even the old and valuable insights which we have inherited from our illustrious ancestors are being drowned in a torrent of meaningless verbiage and useless technicalities.[11]

Such trifling academic research was facilitated in the academic context of a publish-or-perish philosophy, in which research was confused with knowledge, methodology masqueraded as discovery, and pedantry passed for profundity. Not surprisingly, such inanities have become the hallmark of academic dignity. However, in a culture of aimless productivity, even such gimmickry could meet the demand for the accountability of academics and universities. Unfortunately, all this was blindly reinforced by the gullibility of the tax-paying public, as Howard Zinn wryly noted: "Thanks to a gullible public, we have been honored, flattered, even paid for producing the largest number of inconsequential studies in the history of civilization ..., like politicians we have thrived on public innocence."[12] However, in the long run, such a state of affairs proves to have dire consequences for the academic milieu, as two observers of the academic marketplace noted almost four decades ago: "The multiplication of specious and trivial research has some tendency to contaminate the academic atmosphere and to bring knowledge itself into disrepute."[13]

Estimates made by historians of the knowledge enterprise, as well as examinations of the scholarly communication network (such as the citation index), seem to suggest that a considerably large proportion of published studies have negligible merit in terms of impact on the discipline – so that even if a large percentage of academics quit publishing altogether, there would be no loss at all to the scholarly enterprise.[14] While such dispensability rates may vary from one discipline to another, they all seem to be in a fairly high range – which means that a majority of research and scholarly publications contribute more to the pulp and paper industry than to the advancement of knowledge. From which follows the rather sobering and disturbing conclusion that a high proportion of academic success may well be based on negligible merit.

Albeit unspoken, it is also a well-known fact among academics that an average run-of-the-mill publication in scholarly and research journals is read by an average of about half a dozen people – which means that in many cases the average readership of a publication may well be limited to the scholar, researcher, reviewer and an editor who skims through it – not to mention a couple of graduate students who desperately need a few obscure studies to bolster their thesis bibliography. As Rieff noted: "With so many authors who remains behind to read?" So much then for another sacred cow of academia, which tells us that most research published in academic journals is worthwhile, and deserving of rewards and recognition.

Even an administrator-scientist like James Conant, former president of Harvard University, was wary of the tide of "unconnected trivialities" produced by empirical research, and the "trivialities of research" especially in the social sciences – and provided some friendly presidential advice: "The trivial nature and limitations of much of the research of the American social sciences are all too infrequently pointed out. Most of the theses presented for a doctor's degree in some fields would be best left at least unpublished, if not unwritten."[15]

The same may well be said of academic research in almost all other areas. Thus it is not surprising to find Karl Popper taking academic philosophy to task in words that can easily be generalized to much of what goes on in the humanities and the social sciences:

> Criticism is the lifeblood of philosophy, to be sure. Yet we should avoid hairsplitting. A minute criticism of minute points without an understanding of the great problems of cosmology, of human knowledge, of ethics and of political philosophy, and without a serious and devoted attempt to solve them, appears to me fatal. It almost looks as if every printed passage which with some effort might be misunderstood or misinterpreted is good enough to justify the writing of another critical philosophical paper. Scholasticism, in the worst sense of the term, abounds; all the great ideas are buried in a flood of words.[16]

Ironically, then, the growth of knowledge has actually been hampered by the flood of publications generated in the academic context of a publish-or-perish philosophy. Such an anomaly has an obvious explanation, as Barzun observes: "It is safe to say that the steady stream of 'studies' does not really add to the public's knowledge. One report cancels another.... The outcome in fact is that the torrent of books and papers steadily increases the unlikelihood of synthesis.... Minutiae come to look important because they occupy space." Pointing out the role of the computer in encouraging a great deal of research into all sorts of factual trivialities, Barzun rightly questions the assumption underlying all such piecemeal research:

> The assumption here is that a large number of small items, insignificant in themselves, can when added up yield important truths. So far nothing of profound importance has emerged. The interesting work, the great work, continues to be done in the traditional way by men and women who have something to say: they are not simply "doing research."[17]

It is clear that there are limits to unrestrained growth even in the case of research. For, as research continues to expand both the pace and production of information, it makes synthesis all the more unlikely – which increases uncertainty, and inhibits understanding. Thus, massive ignorance may well be the paradoxical outcome of such mass production.

❦— III —❦

Mass production – whether of pins, pocket calculators or pedantic papers – means division of labor and specialization. This Baconian strategy for the advancement of learning is now deeply rooted in the groves of academe, and in all its disciplinary grooves. Universities organized around departments and disciplines have served only to reinforce the specialization strategy and consequently to hinder the integration of knowledge, as Rene Dubos observed a quarter century ago:

> The integration of knowledge cannot readily be achieved within the university structure, which is discipline-oriented and not mission-oriented. Yet, integration of knowledge is essential for achieving a

comprehensive view of the world in which we live, and it is even more important to the world we want to create.[18]

Thus, the departmental academic structure itself serves as a primary obstacle in promoting the integration of knowledge – which is a prime requisite for cultivating intellect. Reinforcing such disciplinary divisions is the analytic research strategy which breeds a host of disciplinary sub-specialisms.

While specialization is the unavoidable consequence of analytical research, specialized knowledge needs to be constantly synthesized into a larger picture so as to provide an integrated and intelligible view of the way things are, and the bearing they have on our view of the world. However, in reality, the gap between analysis and synthesis continues to widen with every increase in the rate and amount of information generated by the omnipresent analytical research. Historian Erich Kahler underlines the perilous consequences that have followed from such a state of affairs:

> The disorganization and at the same time immense proliferation of our learning, and the steady progression of analysis have exerted an unsettling influence on the state of mind of people at large. The impossibility of drawing any meaning from the mass of material and reasoning assembled in our age has given rise to desperate movements, like futurism, Dadaism and surrealism, which … attempted first of all to destroy all meaning wherever it could still be found in the conventional uses of language and action. … Thus, loss of meaning produced disillusionment with illusory meanings, weariness of meaning, intentional destruction of meaning, and ultimate crumbling of meaning and coherence in the very texture of daily life.[19]

To Kahler's list, which includes existentialism, we may also add deconstructionism among the most insidious forms of assault on meaning. Allowing such developments to continue, Kahler believes, "may one day break down the last barriers of civilization." This is a serious cause for concern in higher education which has been infiltrated by all varieties of specialized courses founded on analytical research. For analysis without synthesis has destructive effects on the human mind, as Kahler had warned: "If analysis is carried on exclusively and unrestrictedly, if it lacks the control of organized synthesis, then it is bound to lead into disintegration of our knowledge, our mind, and our very life."[20]

Exclusive and unrestricted analytical research, however, has become so deeply entrenched in the knowledge industry that works of synthesis are not only few and far between, but generally ignored by those engaged in specialized research. Thus, although the specialization strategy seems to have worked well for the natural sciences and some other divisible disciplines, even there it has led to serious communication gaps between academic specialists. As philosopher Stephen Toulmin pointed out: "Within the whole grand enterprise of physics, we seem to be marching bravely down the Road to Babel. The division of labor has fragmented the scientific profession to a point quite disconcerting to the onlooker."[21] With so many researchers claiming to be working at the "cutting edge" it is not surprising that disciplines have been chopped up so badly.

Werner Heisenberg was even more specific about the consequences of specialization:

> Scientists now work as stonemasons did once on cathedrals. They put the stones next to one another with great attention to detail and the work of the fellow next to them, but they have no sense of the architectonics of the whole. And sometimes they do not even have a sense of the purpose of the cathedral.[22]

Yet, such hyper-specialized technician-scientists are the prize products of our age of technology. Aiming for the respectable status enjoyed by such technicians in the natural sciences, academics across the board – in the humanities and the social sciences – have busied themselves with trivial and esoteric territories of their own expertise. While the result of this is a great deal of mumbo-jumbo, it is jargonized enough to make a scholarly impression on rich funding agencies, publicity-conscious administrators, pretentious journal referees, understanding colleagues, innocent students, and the gullible tax-paying public.

Such esoteric curiosities have been parasitic on public funds – which could well serve many more urgent needs of society. However, the generation of much of this specialized nonsense is the result, not only of allowing private curiosity to be satisfied at public expense, but also of gearing research and publications to professional advancement and public status – so that grantsmanship eventually becomes more important than scholarship.

Even where specialization is not abused or exploited, it proves disastrous – purely for intellectual reasons. By knowing more and more about less and less, one actually ends up knowing less, as Mumford had observed. Furthermore, specialization eventually leads to the fragmentation of the mind, for only in the context of the general scheme of knowledge is it possible to have integrated thought. Commenting on the danger of "specialist chaos", Will Durant underlines the predicament of the modern mind:

> ... inductive data fall upon us from all sides like the lava of Vesuvius; we suffocate with uncoordinated facts; our minds are overwhelmed with science breeding and multiplying into specialist chaos for want of synthetic thought and a unifying philosophy. We are all fragments of what a man might be.[23]

Such specialist chaos in academia was clearly the result of an implicit acceptance of the Baconian strategy for the advancement of learning through division of labor – which had worked so well in the organized specialisms of an industrial culture based on mass production. The price of such specialization has been the fragmentation of thought and the destruction of meaning – with consequent disintegration of intellect.

❧— IV —❧

It would be unwise, however, for anyone to deny that there is still a great need for research in all areas relating to the further improvement of the human condition – such as medicine and health, food and agriculture, energy and life-support systems. Even so it may not always be easy to tell when ignorant politicians are being misled by arrogant experts into supporting needless research to serve their common political or career ambitions. Incompetence wedded to pretentiousness is a drain on public funds, which can be more directly used to feed the hungry and clothe the naked.

Likewise, no one can deny the significant role played by science and technology in improving the lot of humanity – even though, in many cases, this has been achieved only at a price. As science has probed ever deeper into the investigation of nature, technology has cut even deeper into all the conditions of human existence. While knowledge has given power, it has given it indiscriminately to the power-thirsty and the profit-hungry, too. A mass devaluation of morality may be the ultimate pric we have to pay for the inflated lifestyle of a technological civilizatior

Morality is indeed the price we have paid in an academic context of inflated research productivity – as is obvious from the many cases of fraud and fudging in scientific research that have been coming to light more and more frequently. It seems obvious that research and publication pressures, along with accountability to bureaucratic administrators and funding agencies, have not only led to superficial results, as Einstein had predicted, but also to a fast growing industry of fraud in research.

With the increasing number of cases of fraud that are coming to our attention, it is obvious that morality has indeed become a victim of an obsession with research. It would therefore not be an overstatement to say that the subject of fraud in research may eventually turn out to be as important a concern as some of the socio-economic-political issues of the day. Nor would it be a case of scaremongering, for what we are dealing with here is the very integrity of the whole knowledge enterprise itself. We cannot therefore afford to pretend that the problem will go away if we simply ignore it. Moreover, such moral lapses in research can no longer be dismissed as insignificant and isolated incidents, since their increase in recent years is closely related to the rather topsy-turvy value system and lop-sided priorities that are currently operating in academic institutions.

Of course, not all cases of fraud in the history of science have resulted either from publication pressures or the need to be accountable. For instance, the need for recognition is a powerful need in science and scholarship – as witnessed in the well-known case of the "discovery" of the Piltdown man (1912), which was shown to be a hoax some forty years later – by which time the creative perpetrator of the hoax had already died with his public prestige intact. Then there is the tragic case of the brilliant evolutionary theorist, Paul Kammerer, who had claimed to have found experimental support for the Lamarckian theory of the inheritance of acquired characteristics (1924). However, when only a few years later his experimental evidence was exposed as fraudulent – apparently due to some tampering by an unscrupulously overenthusiastic research assistant – Kammerer committed suicide, not from any sense of guilt, but from the realization that his whole lifework may have become questionable in the eyes of the scientific world.[24]

On the basis of such historical examples, one may argue that science is self-corrective – that fudging and fraud are eventually exposed. Certainly, the Piltdown man and Kammerer's experimental specimen came under extremely close scrutiny. However, it is important to keep in mind the fact that in both these cases, extremely important issues were at stake, and were hot topics of discussion among leading scholars of the day. Rightly so, since one dealt with the question of the origins of humanity and the missing link controversy, and the other with a mechanism of evolution going beyond the Darwinian theory of natural selection. Thus, whenever research bears on significant theoretical issues, or on novel medical, social or educational practices, it is often subjected to the closest critical scrutiny.

While it is obvious that works of such potential significance would come under critical examination, instances of fudging and fraud are coming to light every now and then – even in the case of high profile researchers and highly funded projects at some of the most prestigious universities.[25] Fortunately, however, their numbers are still relatively low so that the knowledge enterprise as a whole has not been significantly damaged. But even these small number of cases have undermined public confidence to some extent.

It is also becoming clear that the highly trusted peer review system has not always had much success in detecting fraud prior to publication. What is important to note is that if fraud and fudging go on even in highly visible research which is subject to replication and scrutiny, there is no way of determining the extent of the problem, even if it is widely prevalent, in the case of much of the less visible research and the majority of insignificant studies which remain unreplicated or unread. In all empirical/experimental research, based on gathering and analyzing data, the temptation to fudge the results is obviously fuelled by the reward system of grants, tenure, promotion, prestige and other fringe benefits. Perhaps the best example of fraud in the humanities is deconstructionism which has resulted in the generation of publications that border between meaning anything or nothing – and nobody is even supposed to be in a position to judge which is which, except the reader.

It is therefore the academic system, with its perverse emphasis on research 'productivity', which is responsible for producing the kind of pressures that eventually lead to various forms of unethical or nonsensical practices. Is it any wonder, then, that many researchers who are trying to make it in such an academic system find it difficult to resist the temptation to allow their professional lives to be guided by a somewhat liberal interpretation of the biblical commandment to go forth and multiply?

There are obvious lessons to be drawn from such reflections on the blind worship of this high-profile academic dummy that we call research 'productivity' – which has corrupted quality by quantifying it as output. When the pursuit of knowledge becomes so heavily dependent on grants, salesmanship and grantsmanship become far more important than scholarship; when academic fringe benefits depend on productivity, the pursuit of truth becomes secondary to getting results and publications – by hook or by crook; when quantitative considerations become predominant in academic success, quantity of publications becomes far more important than the quality of thought that goes into them. Under these circumstances, everything becomes fair game – from the peddling of old ideas as original discoveries to fraud in research.

On the portals of many sectors of the academic knowledge industry, therefore, the inscription could well read:

Pedantry in Progress, Pursuit of Trivia, Specialists at Busywork, followed by a warning to all those about to enter:

Proceed with Caution, Tunnel-Vision Ahead, Intellect at Risk.

V

It would not be an exaggeration at all to say that the modern university in North America is dedicated to the glorification of mindless research, and to the greater glory of bureaucratic administration – both at the expense of the education of students. Unless we stop worshipping at the altar of academic research and productivity, and substantially decrease the ongoing bureaucratization of education and scholarship, there seems to be little hope that universities can long survive as institutions of higher education. They will simply become post-secondary academies for job training & research.

Pedantry without purpose has only landed us in a blind alley. As Sigmund Koch expressed bluntly: "Research is not knowledge," noting that the "syndrome most widely evident in modern scholarship" is "ameaningful thinking" that "regards knowledge as the result of 'processing' rather than discovery" and "presumes that knowledge is an almost automatic result of a gimmickry, an assembly-line, a methodology." Such ameaningful thought, he observed, has brought about "a grave impasse in the history of scholarship."[26] Undoubtedly, processed knowledge without reflective thought constitutes a serious threat to intellect.

No one who is deeply concerned about the fate of higher education can afford to ignore Mumford's warning:

> As a means for creating an orderly and intelligible world, the automation of knowledge has already come close to bankruptcy. ...
> ... most of our larger academic institutions are as thoroughly automated as a steel-rolling mill or a telephone system: the mass production of scholarly papers, discoveries, inventions, patents, students, Ph.D.'s, professors and publicity ... goes on at a comparable rate; and only those who identify themselves with the goals of the power system, however humanly absurd, are in line for promotion, for big research grants, for the political power and the financial rewards allotted to those who 'go with' the system.[27]

Such academic overproduction, Mumford notes, has had paralyzing effects, making it extremely difficult "to explore the past or keep up with the present," – thus placing both our creativity and rationality at stake. Without self-imposed restraints, he concludes, such an academic culture will most certainly bring about "a state of intellectual enervation and depletion hardly to be distinguished from massive ignorance."[28] Excessive productivity thus places intellect itself at risk.

Already we are soaking in information and technical knowledge, even as we continue thirsting for understanding and wisdom. The information superhighway has no time or place for reflective thought and intellectual life. Ironically, then, the advancement of such technical knowledge and the dissemination of disconnected information have exacted a heavy price in more than one way – a devalued morality, degraded creativity, and a rundown rationality – not to mention a runaway technology. Moreover, if all the research and specialization to date is not to result in the further devaluation of mind, meaning or morality, we will have to become serious about changing some of our general priorities. What we need is a sense of global communion, more than we need improvements in high-tech communication systems; we need a transformation in the quality of our lives more than we need speedier transportation to nowhere; we need, not further information explosion, but a greater wisdom to use the knowledge already at our disposal, along with the courage and determination to work towards elimination of poverty and the promotion of peace.

There is an urgent need, then, for some global thinking about problems that threaten the very survival of our humanized planet. By now, almost everyone knows that population, poverty, pollution and peace are the big-four problems that the twentieth century will have to solve soon – if we are to survive the twenty-first century. However, contrary to what many may believe, these problems will eventually have to be solved, not so much by better technology, further research or greater specialization, as by more good will, fair distribution, commonsense – and a sound liberal education for the citizens and leaders of tomorrow, so that they may temper our runaway technology with reflective thought and good judgement informed by our rich intellectual tradition.

Tradition and technology face in opposite directions. While tradition in the context of education is focused on the preservation of the best that has been thought and said, technology experiments with the bringing into the present of ever new futures. A shared tradition is necessary for the preservation of a sense of community, while a collective only needs common aims to mold a future. In shifting from tradition to technology, modern civilization has become a technological collective based on the awesome power of science and organization. A technological civilization makes demands on the educational system which are different from the demands made by a more tradition based culture. Modern technical and popular cultures represented by technocracy and ideological collectivism are inherently inhospitable to liberal education and thereby promote historical amnesia. However, the stability of liberal education is even more imperative in a rudderless technological civilization which has a tendency to run amok. Thus, liberal education which grounds knowledge in a historical context may be the only way of preserving a healthy balance between tradition and technology, and for preventing the destruction of mind, meaning and memory.

The plight of the individual in a technology-ridden society is well expressed in Ellul's poignant words: "The experience of empty time which we have to fill on our own by conversation, by relations with other people, by reflection or by reading, has become a traumatic one for our generation."[29] Moreover, the invasion of our mental space by the fragmented and decontextualized information provided by the media has destructive effects on memory, as Richard Stivers had noted: "Infatuated with the new and the sensational the media unwittingly destroy the memory of the past."[30] Without memory of the past, we can only move towards barbarism and totalitarianism, as Erich Kahler observed: "The complete victory of totalitarianism would be identical with the complete forgetting of history; that is with a mankind become void of reflection."[31] That is the severe cost of ignoring history.

Recovery from historical amnesia is thus a prime requisite for a sound higher education – so that we may become conversant with the best that has been thought and said over the last two and a half millennia of our rich intellectual history. Even the great Goethe, whose own words and works have an eminent place among the best that has been thought and said, was himself a devotee of such an approach, as his exhortation makes clear:

> Never mind studying contemporaries and those who strive with you. Study the great men of the past, whose works have maintained their value and stature for centuries. A truly gifted mind will naturally so incline; and the desire to delve into the great precursors is the very mark of a higher endowment. Study Molière, study Shakespeare, but above all study the ancient Greeks, ever and always the Greeks.[32]

This is crucial if higher education is to instill a desire to pursue knowledge, understanding and wisdom. For, as Goethe realized, all the truly wise thoughts have already been thought many times, but to make them truly ours, they need to be thought over again honestly until they take root in our own personal experience. Accordingly, such liberal studies are essential if higher education is to lead to wiser living.

However, respecting even the distant historical past means treating our intellectual ancestors, not as remote objects of curiosity and veneration, but as contemporaries with whose thoughts we must come to grips, in order that we may understand not only the very structure and categories of our own thought, but also much of the confusion in modern thought. Beholding the power and wisdom of ancient thought is in itself a humbling experience – worth cultivating for its intrinsic value in maintaining a balanced and informed intellectual perspective.

However, we need to say to the teacher something comparable to what we have long said to the physician: "Teacher, educate thyself!" Perhaps, teachers need to take a "Socratic Oath" to preserve the critical intellectual tradition. Along these lines, Rieff's advice to fellow teachers is most appropriate: "We teachers must produce, first in ourselves, those protections of older wisdom which may help stave off arrogant stupidities parading as originality, modernization, revolution, and, of course, values. Respect for what is long known is not charismatic."[33] Nor is it a luxury for a few esoteric historians – since all significant ideas have a meaningful continuity across the millennia of human history, such that we can build educational bridges between the ideas of the past and the present. As the eminent historian Page Smith put it: "It might well be said that the goal of education is to make students at home in the world by making them at home in history."[34]

Historical understanding is therefore as critical for an individual as it is for an academic discipline. For the individual, ignoring the past means paying the penalty of alienation from the self – since the very fabric of our identity is made up of the threads of our historical past. Self-knowledge and meaning are thus rooted in history, so that we literally discover ourselves in the vast prism of history. Likewise, we could say, with H.G. Wells, that all history is a history of ideas – ideas which are embodied in the best that human beings have thought and said through the ages. A study of the history of ideas, incorporated in liberal education, allows us to witness the perennial issues of human existence, the constants of the human condition, the broad spectrum of human values, and the diverse meanings of human experience. Liberal education thus widens our range of consciousness and elevates our knowledge of the place of humanity in the larger scheme of things – at the same time liberating our minds from the many prejudices of the present, and immunizing us against humbug and collectivist group-think.

Higher education may thus be called 'higher' only to the extent that it enables our minds to behold the heights to which human intellect and imagination have soared during the course of our history. Teachers, therefore, have a prime obligation to transmit to the young the whole intellectual-literary-cultural heritage that informs the knowledge enterprise. For, without a vision of this heritage, intellect can only perish.

What else can become of intellect when so many academics themselves have unwittingly become so unmindful of it as to have already closed their minds to a vision of the university as a temple of intellect – a sanctuary dedicated primarily to the supreme task of fostering a lifelong passion for the pursuit of the intellectual virtues of knowledge, understanding and wisdom, and to the quest for the enduring human values of truth, beauty and goodness.

Widespread amnesia for this deeper meaning and significance of higher education constitutes the current tragedy of academic life.

Epilogue

The moral of quality of a university depends on the intensity and seriousness of its intellectual life.

> — Charles Homer Haskins
> *The Rise of Universities*[1]

For too long have the universities been like melting-pots brewing a hodgepodge of policies and purposes under the combined influence of changing societal trends, fluctuating market demands, the demands of a technological civilization, reformist pressure politics of various interest groups, government demands for accountability, and corporate style thinking. It has become evident now that, over the years, such discordant pressures have resulted in a lethal academic concoction – consisting of the bureaucratization of education, commercialization of knowledge, assembly-line research, hyper-specialization, professional-vocational programs, a market-oriented curriculum, ideologies of victimism, a politically correct agenda, relativism of values, and the nihilism of deconstructionism.

All such developments have cost the university its very identity as a temple of intellect, since they have played a major role in aggravating the fragmentation of the academic mind and the consequent erosion of intellectual life in academia. Without academic and public recognition of the university as a temple of intellect for the pursuit of truth and for the liberation of the human mind from ignorance and prejudice, it would be impossible for the university either to remain an intellectual community of scholars, or to retain the ideal of intellectual and moral integrity.

Only the restoration of intellect via liberal education can provide the coherence and integrity necessary for the cultivation of a life of the mind – which is the ultimate foundation of all human civilization. Thus, if the university is to remain a trustee for civilization, then it is imperative that it serve as a beacon illuminating our intellectual heritage for the enrichment of our moral and spiritual culture – which is the true mission of the university.

Will we allow our academic destiny to be nourished by its traditional roots in the past? Our options are clear. Guided by such a mission of the university, higher education cannot but undergo a renaissance in the twenty-first century. Without such a vision of our intellectual heritage, the true meaning and purpose of higher education will surely fade away into oblivion. We would then have no choice but to observe a prolonged period of silence in memory of the death of Socrates.

References/Notes

References/Notes

1. George Orwell's quotation is from the suppressed *Introduction* to the *Animal Farm*; published by the N.Y. Times, 1972 [cited in George Seldes, *The Great Thoughts*, Ballantine Books, N.Y. 1985; p. 316]

2. Quotation is attributed to the former Harvard President Charles William Eliot. Cited in Richard Norton Smith, *Harvard Century*, (Simon & Schuster, 1986), p. 35

Prologue

1. Claude Bissell's review comment is quoted in *The University Game*, (Anansi, Toronto; 1968), edited by Howard Adelman & Dennis Lee.

Chapter 1:

The Decline and Fall of Higher Education

1. Paul Goodman, *Compulsory Mis-education* and *The Community of Scholars* (Vintage Books, Random House), 1964, p. 325

2. Comment by Heather Cameron, graduate student at York University. Cited in *Maclean's* Special Issue, November 25, 1996, p. 54

3. 'Good education system important for dealing with Canada's crisis' *The Guardian*, Charlottetown, P.E.I., May 27, 1991, pp. 1&3

4. Philip Rieff, *Fellow Teachers* (Dell Publishing, 1972/1973), p. 6

5. Erich Kahler, *The Tower and the Abyss* (Viking Press, 1967), p. 281

6. Lionel Trilling, *Mind in the Modern World* (N.Y. Viking Press, 1972), p. 29

7. I had also used 'historical amnesia' as a quasi-diagnostic term for the state of affairs in academic psychology in my book *The Psychological Quest: From Socrates to Freud* (Captus University Press, North York, 1987; Rev. Ed. 1990). As I had noted at the time, the term is equally applicable to the wider academic scene.

8. Goethe's quotation is from *Goethe's World View, op. cit.*, p. 167

9. All quotations are from Wilhelm von Humboldt, "On the Organization of Institutions of Higher Learning in Berlin' in *The Great Ideas Today* (Encyclopedia Brittanica, 1969), pp. 350-355

10. All quotations are from:
John Henry Newman, *The Scope and Nature of University Education* (E.P. Dutton Inc., 1958).
---- 'The Idea of a University' in *The Great Ideas Today, op.cit.*, 1969, pp. 358-383

11. All quotations are from Thorstein Veblen, *The Higher Learning in America* (Hill & Wang, N.Y., 1918, 1946)

12. All quotations are from:
Robert M. Hutchins, *The Higher Learning in America* (Yale University Press, 1936)
---- *The Learning Society* (New American Library, 1968)
---- *The Great Conversation* (Encyclopedia Brittanica Inc., Chicago, 1952)

Chapter 2:

Illiberal Education & Intellectual Illiteracy

1. Ivan Illich and Barry Saunders, *The Alphabetization of the Popular Mind* (Penguin Books, 1988), p. ix

2. Reference is to E.D. Hirsch Jr., *Cultural Literacy* (Houghton Mifflin Co., 1987). Quotation is from E.D. Hirsch, J.F. Kett, J. Trefil, *The Dictionary of Cultural Literacy* (Houghton Mifflin Company, Boston, 1993), p. xv

3. J. Ortega y Gasset's quotation is from *The Revolt of the Masses*, (W.W. Norton, 1932), p. 107

4. List of Great Ideas is based on Mortimer Adler's *The Great Ideas*, (Macmillan Publishing Co., 1952/1992)

5. Matthew Arnold's definition is from 'The Function of Criticism at the Present Time' in *Critical Theory Since Plato*, ed. H. Adams, 1971

6. Jacques Barzun, *The House of Intellect* (Harper, 1961), p. 122

7. Jacques Ellul, *The Technological Society* (Random House, 1964), p. 349

Alvin Kernan, *The Death of Literature* (Yale University Press, 1990), p. 9

Neil Postman, *Technopoly* (Alfred A. Knopf, 1992), p. 118

10. Harold A. Innis, *The Bias of Communication* (University of Toronto Press, 1951/1968), p. 208

11. John R. Seeley, 'The University as a Slaughterhouse' in *The Great Ideas Today*, 1969, *op. cit.*, p. 75

12. E.F. Schumacher, *Good Work* (Harper & Row, 1979), p. 25

13. Oscar Wilde's quotation is from *The Fireworks of Oscar Wilde*, ed. Owen Dudley Edwards (London, Barrie & Jenkins, 1989), p. 45

14. Richard M. Weaver, *Ideas Have Consequences* (University of Chicago Press, 1948), pp. 136-137

15. Reference is to Arthur Koestler's book *The Call Girls* (Dell Publishing, 1973).

16. Quotation from James A. Perkins is cited in Paul Woodring's book, *The Higher Learning in America: A Reassessment* (McGraw-Hill, 1968), p. 22

17. Quotation is from William J. Bennett's Address at Harvard University, Cambridge, Massachusetts, October 10, 1986, p. 16

18. Robert M. Hutchins, *Freedom, Education and the Fund* (Meridian Books, 1956), p. 165

19. Mortimer J. Adler, *Reforming Education* (Macmillan Publishing Co., 1988), p. xxxi

20. Quoted in Will Durant, *Rosseau and Revolution*, Vol. X of *The Story of Philosophy* (Simon & Schuster, 1967), p. 551

21. M. Mujeeb Rahman, *The Psychological Quest, op. cited.* Evidence for the modernity of the ancients is amply demonstrated in the discussion on the contributions of the ancient Greeks to psychological thought.

22. Michael Oakeshott, *The Voice of Liberal Learning* (Yale University Press, 1989), p. 101

23. Philip Rieff, *Fellow Teachers, op. cit.*, p. 39

24. Paul Woodring, *op. cit.*, p. 182

25. Richard Stivers, *The Culture of Cynicism* (Blackwell Publishers, Cambridge, 1994), p. 59

26. Mortimer Adler, *A Guidebook to Learning* (Macmillan, N.Y. 1986), p. 146-147

27. Jeremy Rifkin, *Entropy* (Bantam Books, 1981) p. 170

28. John Ralston Saul, *Voltaire's Bastards* (Penguin, Toronto, 1993), p. 476

29. Arthur Schlesinger, Jr., *The Disuniting of America* (W.W. Norton & Co., 1992), p. 99, p. 102

30. Harold A. Innis, *op. cit.*, p. 133

31. Cited in Robert M. Hutchins, *The Great Conversation* (Chicago, Encyclopedia Brittanica, 1952), p. 71

32. Cited in Robert M. Hutchins, *The Great Conversation*, *op. cit.*, p. 72

33. Cited in Robert M. Hutchins, *The Great Conversation*, *op. cit.*, p. 70

34. Bruce Cole and Ahelheid Gealt, *Art of the Western World* (Simon & Schuster, 1989), p. vii [Michaelangelo's view is presented in William Fleming, *Arts and Ideas* (Holt, Rinehart & Winston, 3rd ed.) p. 287]

35. Thomas Cleary, *Living a Good Life* (Shambhala, 1997), p. vii

36. Jacques Barzun, Western Civ. or Western Sieve? in J. Barzun, *Begin Here, The Forgotten Conditions of Teaching and Learning* (University of Chicago Press, 1991), p. 131

37. Roger Kimball, *Tenured Radicals: How Politics Has Corrupted Our Higher Education* (Harper & Row, 1991), pp. 197-198

38. Riane Eisler, *The Chalice & the Blade* (HarperCollins, 1995), p. 142

39. G. Lloyd Evans, *The Upstart Crow, An Introduction to Shakespeare's Plays* (London, J.M. Dent & Sons Ltd.), 1982, pp. 74-75

40. Marilyn French, *Shakespeare's Division of Experience* (Random House, 1981), p. 349

41. Juliet Mitchell, *Psychoanalysis and Feminism* (Vintage Books, Random House, 1974), p. xiii

42. Norman Brown, *Life Against Death* (Random House, 1959), pp. xi-xii

43. In *The Book of J*, Trans. David Rosenberg, interpreted by Harold Bloom, (Grove Weidenfeld, N.Y., 1990)

44. Quotation of Georgia O'Keefe is cited in Laurence Boldt, *Zen and the Art of Living* (Penguin Books, 1993), p. 30

45. Camille Paglia, *Sexual Personae* (Vintage Books, Random House, 1985), p. 169

46. Cited in *The Great Thoughts*, ed. George Seldes, (Ballantine Books, 1985), p. 169

Chapter 3:

The Academic Assault on Intellect

1. Jacques Barzun's quotation is from his Foreword to Theodore Caplow & Reese McGee, *The Academic Marketplace* (Anchor Books, 1965), p. vi

2. Quotations of Irving Howe and H. Stuart Hughes are from Russell Jacoby, *The Last Intellectuals: American Culture in the Age of Academe* (The Noonday Press, Farrar, Straus and Giroux, 1987), pp. 82 and 72

3. Robert M. Hutchins, *The Higher Learning in America* (Yale University Press, 1936), p. 27

4. Philip Rieff, *Fellow Teachers*, *op. cit.*, pp. 8-94

5. Alvin Kernan, *The Death of Literature* (Yale University Press, 1990), p. 2

6. Sidney Hook, *Academic Freedom and Academic Anarchy* (Dell Publishing Co., 1969), pp. 121-122 and p. xiii

7. From A.M. Sullivan, *The Three Dimensional Man* (P.J. Kennedy & Sons, 1956). Cited in *Toward the Liberally Educated Executive*, ed. Robert Goldwin & Charles Nelson, (New American Library, 1960), p. 70

8. Philip Rieff, *Fellow Teachers, op. cit.*, p. 6

9. J. Paul Getty, *How To Be A Successful Executive* (Chicago, Playboy Press, 1971), pp. 75-76, 79

10. Louis Wirth's quotation is from Edward H. Levi, 'The University As Custodian of Reason' in *The Great Ideas Today*, ed. Robert M. Hutchins and Mortimer J. Adler, *op. cit.*, 1969, p. 36

11. Albert Schweitzer, 'Reverence for Life' in *A Treasury of Albert Schweitzer*, ed. Thomas Kierman (Gramercy Books, 1994), p. 219

12. Sigmund Freud, 'Why War?' (1932) in *The Collected Papers of Sigmund Freud*, ed. Philip Rieff (Crowell-Collier, 1963), p. 147

13. Sigmund Freud, *The Future of an Illusion*, trans. J. Strachey, (W.W. Norton, 1961), p. 53

14. John Kenneth Galbraith, *The New Industrial State* (New American Library, 1967), p. 73

15. G. Bernard Shaw, *Man and Superman* (Penguin Books, 1946), p. 254

16. Carl Bernstein's article in *The New Republic* reproduced in The Gl and Mail, May 30, 1992, p. D-5

17. Quotation of Edward Shils is taken from Daniel Bell, *The Reforming of General Education* (Anchor Books, 1968), p. 300

18. Alfred North Whitehead, *Science and the Modern World* (The Free Press, 1967), pp. 196-197

19. Albert Einstein, "The Common Language of Science" in *Ideas and Opinions*: Einstein (Dell Publishing, 1954), p. 328

20. Viktor Frankl, Chapter on Reductionism and Nihilism, in Arthur Koestler & J.R. Smythies (eds.), *Beyond Reductionism*, London, 1969

21. Friedrich Nietzsche, *Twilight of the Idols*, in The Portable Nietzsche, trans. Walter Kaufman, (Random House, 1967), pp. 508

22. Ibid., p. 510

23. Philip Rieff, *Fellow Teachers, op. cit.,* p. 96

24. Jacques Barzun, *Teacher in America* (Doubleday Anchor Books, 1954), pp. 222-223

25. Philip Rieff, *Fellow Teachers, op. cit.*, p. 15

26. Jacques Barzun, *Teacher in America, op. cit.,* p. 84

27. William Kearney, *The Wake of Imagination* (London, Hutchinson, 1988). Foucault's views and words appear on pp. 267, 271

28. In 'Michel Foucault' by Mark Philp, in *The Return of Grand Theory in the Human Sciences*, ed. Q. Skinner (Cambridge University Press, 1985) p. 67

29. Stanley Rosen, *The Ancients and the Moderns* (Yale University Press, 1989), p. 20

30. Daniel Bell's quotation is from Rieff, *op. cit.,* p. 129

31. Camille Paglia, *Sex, Art and American Culture* (Vintage Books, 1992), p. 174

32. Goya's quotation is from *The World of Goya* (Time-Life Books, N.Y., 1968), p. 109

33. [*Roland Barthes (1977), **Jacques Derrida (1976), *** Michel Foucault (1979)]. Cited in Pauline Marie Roseneau, *Post-Modernism and the Social Sciences*, (Princeton University Press, 1992), pp. 29-30

34. Herbert London, cited in Antonio T. de Nicolas, *The Habits of the Mind*(Paragon House, 1989), p. pp. xiii-xiv

⁻. George Orwell, "Politics and the English Language", in *Inside the Whale and Other Essays*: Orwell (Penguin Books, 1960), p. 157

36. Stanley Fish, 'The Common Touch' in *The Politics of Liberal Education*, ed. Darryl J. Gless and Barbara H. Smith, (Durham, Duke University Press, 1992), p. 265

37. Pauline Marie Roseneau, *op. cit.*, pp. 55 and 86

38. Gerald Graff, 'Teach the Conflicts' in *The Politics of Liberal Education, op. cit.,* p. 67

39. Reference here is to Dinesh D'Souza, *Illiberal Education* (Vintage Books, Random House, 1991)

40. Richard Stivers, *The Culture of Cynicism, op. cit.*, p. 163

41. Jacques Ellul's quotation appears in Richard Stivers, *The Culture of Cynicism, op. cit.*, p. 151

42. Clarence Randall, 'The Cultivated Mind' in *Toward the Liberally Educated Executive*, ed. Robert A. Goldwin and Charles A. Nelson, *op. cit.,* p. 121

43. Antonio T. de Nicolas, *The Habits of the Mind, op. cit.*, p. 13

44. Harold Innis, *The Bias of Communication* (University of Tornoto Press, 1951), p. 208

45. Paul Tabori, *The Natural History of Stupidity* (Barnes & Noble, N.Y., 1993), p. 100

46. John Seeley, 'The University as Slaughterhouse' in *The Great Ideas Today*, 1969, *op. cit.*, p. 78

47. Page Smith, *Killing the Spirit* (Penguin Books, 1990), p. 298

Chapter 4:

The Closing of the Academic Mind

1. Robert M. Hutchins, *The Learning Society* (New American Library, 1968), p. 131

2. Charles J. Sykes, *Profscam: Professors and the Demise of Higher Education* (St. Martin's Press, 1988), pp. 4-5

3. Quotation from John Maynard Keynes cited in *A Little Learning is a Dangerous Thing*, ed. James Charlton, (St. Martin's Press, 1994), p. 26

4. Robert M. Hutchins, *The Learning Society, op. cit.*, p. 140

5. Francis Bacon, *The Complete Essays* including *The New Atlantis and Novum Organum*, (Washington Square Press, 1963), pp. 203, 257, 68

6. Paul Woodring, *The Higher Learning in America: A Reassessment*, (McGraw-Hill, 1968), p. 188

7. Paul Woodring, ibid., p. 120

8. Camille Paglia, *Sex, Art and American Culture, op. cit.*, pp. 207-208

9. Jacques Barzun, *The American University* (University of Chicago Press, 1968/1993), p. 252

10. Reference is to Edward Said, *Representations of the Intellectual* (Vintage Books, Random House, 1994). Said has used a much broader social-functional conception of the intellectual as one who is "a thinking and concerned member of society" … "fueled by care and affection" rather than by profit, power and narrow specialization (p. 82). However, he seems to see the specialist as simply another representation of the intellectual, except that he sees such a "fully specialized intellectual" as one who succumbs to the conformist pressures of professionalization (p. 77). In my view, an intellectual is quintessentially an individualist with a high degree of immunity to conformist pressures and group-think.

11. John Horgan, *The End of Science* (Addison-Wesley Publishing Company, Inc., 1996)

12. Karl Popper, *In Search of A Better World* (Routledge, London, 1992), p. 62

13. Paul Woodring, *op. cit.*, p. 191

14. Cited in Philip Marchand, *Marshall McLuhan: The Medium and the Messenger* (Vintage Books, Random House, Toronto, 1989), p. 154

15. Friedrich Nietzsche, *The Gay Science*, trans. Walter Kaufmann, N.Y. Random House, 1974), p. 201

16. Northrop Frye, *Spiritus Mundi* (Indiana University Press, 1976), p. 35

7. Quotation of Walt Whitman is from 'Notes Left Over' in *The Collected Writings of Walt Whitman, Prose Works 1892*, Vol. II, ed. Floyd Stovall (New York University Press, 1964), p. 521

. The "Dr. Myron Fox" experiment is reported in Thomas Szasz, 'The Lying Truths of Psychiatry' in *Lying Truths*, compiled by R. Duncan and M. Weston-Smith, (Pergamon Press, 1979), p. 139

19. Aristotle, *Ethics,* in *The Philosophy of Aristotle*, ed. Richard Bambrough, trans. A.E. Wardman and J.L. Creed, (New American Library, 1963), p. 287

20. Jacques Barzun, *Teacher in America* (Doubleday Anchor Books, 1954), p. 166

21. Margaret Mead's quotation is from *A Little Learning is a Dangerous Thing*, ed. James Charlton, *op. cit.,* p. 65

22. Peter Drucker's quotation is from *A Little Learning is a Dangerous Thing,* ibid., p. 65

23. Thomas Szasz's quotation is from *A Little Learning is a Dangerous Thing,* ibid., p. 93

24. Quotation *r* from Williams Blake's poem "Jerusalem" [Chapter 4, plate 91], in *The Complete Poetry & Prose of William Blake*, ed. David Erdman (Doubleday/Anchor Books, 1982), p. 252

25. Pierre Van den Berghe, *Academic Gamesmanship* (Abelard/Schumann), p. 81. Cited in Charles Sykes, *Profscam, op. cit.*, p. 76

26. Herbert London, in Introduction to Jacques Barzun, *The American University, op. cit.*, p. xiii

27. Robert Proctor, *Education's Great Amnesia* (Indiana University Press, 1988), p. 196

28. Thorstein Veblen, *The Higher Learning in America, op. cit.*, p. 186

29. Paul Goodman, *The Community of Scholars, op. cit.*, p. 226

30. Thorstein Veblen, *op. cit.*, p. 202

31. Eric Hoffer, *The Ordeal of Change* (Harper & Row, 1963), p. 47

32. Edward Said, *op. cit.*, p. 82

33. Page Smith, *Killing the Spirit* (Penguin, 1990), p. 179

34. Jacques Barzun, *Teacher in America, op. cit.*, p. 179

Chapter 5:

The Malady of the Academic Knowledge Industry

Some of the points and passages in this chapter are taken from the introductory chapter of my previous book, *The Psychological Quest: From Socrates to Freud, op. cit.*, pp. 12-19. I did not see any need or reason to use different expressions especially in articulating essentially similar thoughts on the subject of research. Undeniably, some degree of intellectual inertia is also involved in such replication.

1. Philip Rieff, *Fellow Teachers, op. cit.*, p. 12

2. Karl Popper, *In Search of a Better World,* London, Routledge, 1992, p. 62

3. Erich Kahler, *The Tower and the Abyss, op. cit.*, p. 47

4. Cited in Derek de Solla Price, *Science since Babylon* (Yale University Press, 1975), p. 93

5. Albert Einstein's quotation is from *Einstein: The Human Side*, ed. Helen Dukas and Banesh Hoffmann, (Princeton University Press, 1979), p. 50

6. Philip Rieff, *Fellow Teachers, op. cit.*, p. 162n

7. David Daube's view cited in Philip Rieff, ibid., p. 154n

8. Lewis Mumford, *The Pentagon of Power* (Harcourt, Brace and Jovanovich, 1970), p. 181

9. Teilhard de Chardin used the term "noosphere" to refer to what he called the "thinking envelope of the Earth" in *The Future of Man* (Collins, London, 1964), p. 137

10. Lewis Mumford, *In the Name of Sanity* (Harcourt, Brace & Co., 1954), p. 50

11. Stanislav Andreski, *Social Science as Sorcery*, (London, Andre Deutsch, 1972), p. 11

12. Howard Zinn, The Politics of History cited in Herbert Livesey, *The Professors* (Charterhouse, N.Y., 1975), p. 233

13. Theodore Caplow and Reese McGee, *The Academic Marketplace* (Doubleday Anchor Books, 1965), p. 190

14. Reference is to a study by Myers (1970) reported by Paul Meehl, Theory and Practice: Reflections of An Academic Clinician, in E.F. Bourg, et al.(Eds.), Standards and Evaluation in the *Education and Training of Professional Psychologists* (Transcript Press, Oklohoma, 1987), p. 17

15. James B. Conant, *Two Modes of Thought* (Pocket Cardinal, 1965), p. 94-95

16. Karl Popper, *In Search of A Better World, op. cit.*, p. 185

17. Jacques Barzun, "Doing Research" – Should the Sport be Regulated? in *Begin Here, op. cit.*, p. 174

18. Rene Dubos, *Reason Awake: Science for Man* (Columbia University Press, 1970), p. 253

19. Erich Kahler, *The Tower and the Abyss, op. cit.*, p. 262-263

20. Ibid., p. 263

21. Stephen Toulmin, 'The Physical Sciences' in *The Great Ideas Today 1967*, ed. Robert M. Hutchins and Mortimer Adler (Encyclopedia Brittanica Inc., 1967), p. 160

22. Werner Heisenberg's quotation could not be retrieved from the deep recesses of electronic memory, and the passage of time has effaced the source of this citation from my far less deeper human memory.

23. Will Durant, *The Story of Philosophy* (Simon & Schuster, 1961), p. 91

24. Both cases are discussed in Curtis MacDougall, *Hoaxes* (Dover Publications, 1958), pp. 208-209. The Paul Kammerer case is discussed fully in Arthur Koestler, *The Case of the Midwife Toad*, Pan Books Ltd., London, 1971).

25. Several recent cases of fraud in scientific research are fully documented in Robert Bell, *Impure Science* (John Wiley & Sons Inc., New York, 1992); and Beth Savan, *Science Under Siege* (CBC Enterprises. Toronto, 1988).

26. Sigmund Koch, 'Psychology Cannot be a Coherent Science' in *Psychology Today* (CRM, 1969), pp. 14, 66-68

27. Lewis Mumford, *The Pentagon of Power, op. cit.*, pp. 181-182

28. Lewis Mumford, *In the Name of Sanity, op. cit.*, p. 50

29. Jacques Ellul quotation is from Richard Stivers, *The Culture of Cynicism, op. cit.*, p. 155

30. Richard Stivers, *The Culture of Cynicism*, ibid., p. 114

31. Erich Kahler, *The Tower and the Abyss, op. cit.*, p. 66

32. Goethe's quotation is from *Goethe's World View, op. cit.*, p. 167

33. Philip Rieff, *Fellow Teachers, op. cit.*, p. 24

34. Page Smith, *Killing the Spirit, op. cit.*, p. 258

Epilogue

1. Charles Homer Haskins, *The Rise of Universities* (Cornell University Press, 1923/1957), p. 91

Index

Name Index

Name Index

Subject Index

Academic
    accountability, 12, 127, 138
    administration, 120, 140
    decision-making, 7, 38, 120
    identity, 8-9
    leadership, 7
'Academic Man' (Sykes), 97
academic Trojan Horse, 45
academic activism, 69-70
Aesop's fables, 58
African studies, 55
American model, 19
ancient and modern, 49, 151
anti-intellectualism, 7, 25, 29
anti-intellectual university, 67, 76
area studies, 55
art, 64
Asian studies, 55, 98
assembly-line training, 13

Bachelor's degree, 15
Baconian methodology, 99, 134, 137
barbarism, 50, 142
'barbarism of specialization', 99
Bhagvad Gita, 65
Bible, 62, 64
British model, 18, 19
Buddhism, 62
bureaucracy, 7, 8, 41, 92, 93, 120,
    128, 140

Call Girls, The (Koestler), 44
Cambridge University, 18
Canadian studies, 55, 98

centers of excellence, 91
citation index, 132
Closing of the American Mind, The, xi
collectivism, 41, 65, 144
Columbia University, 18, 111
commercialism, 5, 128, 145
community of scholars, 104, 120,
    121, 124, 145
Confessions of St. Augustine, 61
Confucian *Aphorisms*, 65
corporate thinking, 93, 127
critical thinking, 1, 3, 5, 7, 41, 67
cultivation of intellect, 17, 18, 34, 74
culture of humanity, 27

Dadaism, 86
Darwinian theory, 139
deconstructionism, 65, 83-86, 106,
    135
'death of literature', 36
departmentalism, 29, 134, 135
doctoral degrees, 15, 79
doctrine of progress, 25
Doric architecture, 62
"Dr. Myron Fox" experiment, 109

Eastern civilization and contributions,
    57, 59, 60
egalitarianism, 52, 54, 70
elective systems, 18, 37, 118
electronic universities, 117
elitism, 11, 99
Elizabethan age, 62
empiricism, 25, 27, 29, 32, 68

Acknowledgments

Grateful acknowledgment is made to the following publishers and authors for permission to use brief excerpts from their publications noted below:

Antonio T. De Nicolas : Excerpt from *Habits of the Mind* by Antonio T de Nicolas. Copyright © 1989 by Antonio T De Nicolas. Published by Paragon House. Reprinted by permission of author.

Blackwell Publishers: Excerpts from *The Culture of Cynicism* by Richard Stivers. Copyright © 1994 by Richard Stivers. Reprinted by permission of publisher.

Columbia University Press: Excerpt from *Reason Awake* by Rene Dubos. Copyright © 1970 by Columbia University Press. Reprinted with permission of the publisher.

Encyclopædia Brittanica: Excerpts from *The Great Conversation* by Robert M. Hutchins. Copyright © 1952 by Encyclopædia Brittanica; *The Learning Society* by Robert M. Hutchins. Copyright © 1968 by Encyclopædia Brittanica. Reprinted with permission of Encyclopædia Britannica, Inc. Excerpts from the following articles in *The Great Ideas Today 1969* edited by Robert M. Hutchins & Mortimer Adler. Copyright © Encyclopædia Britannica, Inc. 1969: 'On the Organization of Institutions of Higher Learning in Berlin' by Wilhelm von Humboldt; 'The Idea of A University' by John Henry Newman; 'The University as a Custodian of Reason' by Edward H. Levi; 'The University as a Slaughterhouse' by John Seeley. Copyright © 1969 by Encyclopædia Britannica. Reprinted with permission of Encyclopædia Britannica, Inc.

Frederick Ungar Publishing Co., Inc.: *Goethe's World View* Edited by Frederick Ungar; translated by Heinz Norden. Copyright © 1963 Frederick Ungar Publishing Co., Inc.

Bantam, Doubleday & Dell/Cowles Book Co., Inc.: Excerpts from *Academic Freedom and Academic Anarchy* by Sidney Hook. Copyright © 1969, 1970 by Sidney Hook. Delta Book/ published by arrangement with Cowles Book Co., Inc.
Bantam, Doubleday & Dell/Little, Brown & Company: Excerpts from *Teacher in America* by Jacques Barzun. Copyright © 1944, 1945 by Jacques Barzun. Doubleday Anchor Book, 1954, published by arrangement with Little, Brown & Company.
Bantam, Doubleday & Dell/The Viking Press: Excerpt from *Entropy* by Jeremy Rifkin. Copyright © 1980 Foundation on Economic Trends. Bantam Book/published by arrangement with The Viking Press.
Bantam, Doubleday & Dell/Harper & Row Publishers, Inc.: Excerpts from *Fellow Teachers* by Philip Rieff. Copyright © 1972, 1973 by Philip Rieff. Delta Book. Reprinted by arrangement with Harper & Row, Publishers, Inc.

HarperCollins: Excerpts from *Fellow Teachers* by Philip Rieff. Copyright © 1972, 1973 by Philip Rieff. Excerpt from *The Ordeal of Change* by Eric Hoffer. Copyright © 1963 by Eric Hoffer. Excerpt from *Tenured Radicals* by Roger Kimball. Copyright © 1991 by Roger Kimball. Reprinted by permission of HarperCollins Publishers, Inc. Excerpt from *Good Work* by E.F. Schumacher. Copyright © 1979 by Verena Schumacher. Reprinted by permission of Verena Schumacher and HarperCollins Publishers, Inc.

Harcourt, Brace & Co.: Excerpts from *The Myth of the Machine: The Pentagon of Power, Volume II* by Lewis Mumford. Copyright © by Lewis Mumford 1964, 1970. Published by Harcourt Brace Jovanovich, Inc. Reprinted by permission of publisher.

Acknowledgments

Houghton Mifflin Co.: Excerpt from *The New Industrial State*, Copyright © 1967 by John Kenneth Galbraith. Excerpt from *The Dictionary of Cultural Literacy* by Hirsch, Kett, Trefil. Copyright © 1988 by Houghton Mifflin Company. Reprinted by permission of Houghton Mifflin Company. All rights reserved.

Indiana University Press: Excerpt from *Education's Great Amnesia* by Robert Proctor. Copyright © 1988 by Robert Proctor. Reprinted by permission of the Indiana University Press.

McGraw Hill Co.: Excerpts from *The Higher Learning in America: A Reassessment* by Paul Woodring. Copyright © 1968 by Paul Woodring. Reprinted with permission of The McGraw Hill Companies.

W.W. Norton & Co., Inc.: Excerpts from *The Disuniting of America* by Arthur Schlesigner Jr. Copyright © 1991, 1992 by Arthur Schlesinger Jr. Reprinted by permission of publisher.

Penguin Books USA Inc.: Excerpts from *Killing the Spirit* by Page Smith. Copyright © 1990 by Page Smith. Excerpts from the "Twilight of the Idols" by Friedrich Nietzsche, edited by Walter Kaufmann, from *The Portable Nietzsche* by Walter Kaufmann, editor, translated by Walter Kaufmann. Translation copyright 1954 by The Viking Press, renewed © 1982 by Viking Penguin Inc. Used by permission of Viking Penguin, a division of Penguin Books USA Inc. Excerpts from *The Tower And The Abyss* by Erich Kahler. Copyright © Erich Kahler 1967. Published by The Viking Press, Inc. by arrangement with George Braziller, Inc. *The Mind in the Modern World* by Lionel Trilling. Copyright © 1972 by Lionel Trilling. Published by the Viking Press. Excerpts from *The Higher Learning in America* by Thorstein Veblen. Copyright © 1918 by B.W. Huebsch. Copyright renewed 1946 by Ann B. Sims. Reprinted by arrangement with the Viking Press. Excerpt from *Entropy* by Jeremy Rifkin. Copyright © 1980 by Foundation on Economic Trends. Published by The Viking Press. Excerpts from *The Scope and Nature of University Education* by John Henry Newman. Published 1958 by E.P. Dutton & Co. Inc.

The Berkley Publishing Group: Excerpt from *How to be a Successful Executive* by J. Paul Getty. Copyright © 1971 by Playboy. Reprinted by permission granted by The Berkley Publishing Group. All rights reserved.

Princeton University Press: *Post-Modernism and the Social Sciences* by Pauline Marie Roseneau. Copyright © 1992 Princeton University Press.

Random House, Inc: Excerpt from *The Technological Society* by Jacques Ellul. Copyright © 1964 by Alfred A. Knopf, Inc. Excerpt from *Psychoanalysis and Feminism* by Juliet Mitchell. Copyright © 1974 by Juliet Mitchell. Excerpts from *Sex, Art, and American Culture* by Camille Paglia. Copyright © 1992 by Camille Paglia. Excerpts from *Shakespeare's Division of Experience* by Marilyn French. Copyright © 1981 by Marilyn French. Reprinted by permission of Random House, Inc.

Regnery Publishing, Inc.: Excerpt from *Profscam* by Charles J. Sykes. Copyright © 1988 by Regnery Publishing. All rights reserved. Reprinted by special permission of Regnery Publishing, Inc., Washington, D.C.

Routledge, Ltd.: Excerpt from *In Search of A Better World* by Karl Popper. Copyright © by Karl R. Popper. Reprinted by permission of the publisher.

Shambhala: Excerpt from *Living a Good Life* translated by Thomas Cleary. Copyright © 1997 by Thomas Cleary. Reprinted by arrangement with Shambhala Publications, Inc., 300 Massachusetts Avenue, Boston, MA. 02115

Acknowledgments

Simon & Schuster: Excerpt from *The Story of Philosophy* by Will Durant. Copyright © 1961 by Will Durant. Excerpt from *Art of the Western World* by Bruce Cole & Adelheid Gealt. Copyright © 1989 by Educational Broadcasting Corporation, Bruce Cole and Adelheid Gealt. Excerpts from *A Guidebook to Learning* by Mortimer Adler. Copyright © 1986 by Mortimer Adler. Excerpts from *Reforming Education* by Mortimer Adler. Copyright © 1988 by Mortimer Adler. Reprinted with the permission of Simon & Schuster. Excerpts from *Science and the Modern World* by Alfred North Whitehead. Copyright © 1925 by Macmillan Publishing Co.; copyright renewed © 1953 by Evelyn Whitehead. Reprinted with the permission of Simon & Schuster.

University of Chicago Press: Excerpt from *Ideas Have Consequences* by Richard Weaver. Copyright © 1948 by The University of Chicago. Excerpt from *The American University* by Jacques Barzun. Copyright © 1968, 1993 by Jacques Barzun. Excerpts from *Begin Here* by Jacques Barzun. Copyright © 1991 The University of Chicago. Reprinted by permission of University of Chicago Press.

University of Toronto Press: *The Bias of Communication* by Harold Innis. Copyright © 1951 University of Toronto Press. Reprinted by permission of the University of Toronto Press.

Yale University Press: Excerpts from *The Higher Learning in America* by Robert Maynard Hutchins. Copyright © 1936 by Yale University Press. Excerpts from *The Voice of Liberal Learning* by Michael Oakeshott. Copyright © 1989 by Yale University. Excerpts from *The Death of Literature* by Alvin Kernan. Copyright © 1990 by Yale University. Excerpt from *Sexual Personae* by Camille Paglia. Copyright © 1990 by Yale University. Reprinted by permission of Yale University Press.

Front cover painting: *The Death of Socrates* by Jacques Louis David. The Metropolitan Museum of Art, Catherine Lorillard Wolfe Collection, Wolfe Fund, 1931. (31.45). Photograph © 1995 The Metropolitan Museum of Art. Reproduced by courtesy of The Metropolitan Museum of Art.

The author deeply regrets any inadvertent errors or omissions in the above list despite every effort made to contact and credit all copyright holders. Sincerest apologies are extended to any publishers or authors who may not have been duly acknowledged due to errors in transcription, inaccuracies in attribution, or delays in notification.

Author Photo credit: Ron Eckroth

Indexing credit: Asifa Rahman

Typesetting credit: Roberta MacLean, TechnoMedia Inc.

About the Author

Mohammed Mujeeb Rahman was born in Hyderabad, India in 1937. He studied at St. Xavier's College, and received his Master's degree in Psychology from the Bombay University in 1961. He was Lecturer in Psychology at Osmania University until 1967, when he received a Fulbright & U.S. State Department Scholarship for higher studies in the U.S. He earned his Ph.D. in Psychology from the University of New Mexico in 1970. He then moved to Canada, and was Professor of Psychology at the University of Prince Edward Island until his retirement in 1997. He has previously published two books: *The Freudian Paradigm: Psychoanalysis & Scientific Thought* (Nelson-Hall, 1977), and *The Psychological Quest: From Socrates to Freud* (Captus University Publications, 1987, 1990).

He is married and has two children. Prince Edward Island has been his imaginary homeland since 1970.